BENJAMIN FRANKLIN

Revolutionary Inventor

Maria Mihalik Higgins

STERLING

New York / London
www.sterlingpublishing.com

For my mother: How much do you want to bet that
Emmy makes it three for three? —M. M. H.

Library of Congress Cataloging-in-Publication Data

Higgins, Maria Mihalik.
 Benjamin Franklin : revolutionary inventor / Maria Mihalik Higgins.
    p. cm. -- (Sterling biographies)
 Includes bibliographical references and index.
 ISBN-13: 978-1-4027-4952-0
 ISBN-10: 1-4027-4952-X
 1. Franklin, Benjamin, 1706-1790--Juvenile literature. 2. Statesmen--United States--Biography-
-Juvenile literature. 3. Inventors--United States--Biography--Juvenile literature. 4. Scientists--
United States--Biography--Juvenile literature. 5. Printers--United States--Biography--Juvenile
literature. I. Title.

E302.6.F8H54 2007
973.3092--dc22
[B]
                                                    2007003629
10 9 8 7 6 5 4 3 2 1

Published by Sterling Publishing Co., Inc.
387 Park Avenue South, New York, NY 10016
© 2007 by Maria Mihalik Higgins
Distributed in Canada by Sterling Publishing
c/o Canadian Manda Group, 165 Dufferin Street
Toronto, Ontario, Canada M6K 3H6
Distributed in the United Kingdom by GMC Distribution Services
Castle Place, 166 High Street, Lewes, East Sussex, England BN7 1XU
Distributed in Australia by Capricorn Link (Australia) Pty. Ltd.
P.O. Box 704, Windsor, NSW 2756, Australia

Printed in China
All rights reserved

Sterling ISBN-13: 978-1-4027-3283-6 (paperback)
        ISBN-10: 1-4027-3283-X
Sterling ISBN-13: 978-1-4027-4952-0 (hardcover)
        ISBN-10: 1-4027-4952-X

Designed by Laura Fields for Simonsays Design!
Image research by Susan Schader

For information about custom editions, special sales, premium and
corporate purchases, please contact Sterling Special Sales
Department at 800-805-5489 or specialsales@sterlingpub.com.

CONTENTS

Events in the Life of Benjamin Franklin

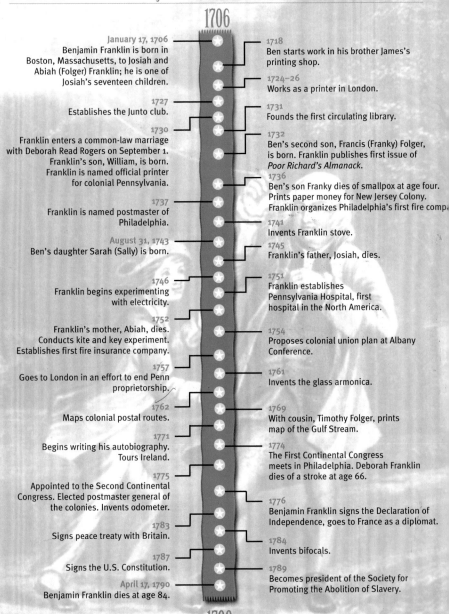

1706

January 17, 1706
Benjamin Franklin is born in Boston, Massachusetts, to Josiah and Abiah (Folger) Franklin; he is one of Josiah's seventeen children.

1718
Ben starts work in his brother James's printing shop.

1724–26
Works as a printer in London.

1727
Establishes the Junto club.

1731
Founds the first circulating library.

1730
Franklin enters a common-law marriage with Deborah Read Rogers on September 1. Franklin's son, William, is born. Franklin is named official printer for colonial Pennsylvania.

1732
Ben's second son, Francis (Franky) Folger, is born. Franklin publishes first issue of *Poor Richard's Almanack*.

1736
Ben's son Franky dies of smallpox at age four. Prints paper money for New Jersey Colony. Franklin organizes Philadelphia's first fire comp

1737
Franklin is named postmaster of Philadelphia.

1741
Invents Franklin stove.

August 31, 1743
Ben's daughter Sarah (Sally) is born.

1745
Franklin's father, Josiah, dies.

1746
Franklin begins experimenting with electricity.

1751
Franklin establishes Pennsylvania Hospital, first hospital in the North America.

1752
Franklin's mother, Abiah, dies. Conducts kite and key experiment. Establishes first fire insurance company.

1754
Proposes colonial union plan at Albany Conference.

1757
Goes to London in an effort to end Penn proprietorship.

1761
Invents the glass armonica.

1762
Maps colonial postal routes.

1769
With cousin, Timothy Folger, prints map of the Gulf Stream.

1771
Begins writing his autobiography. Tours Ireland.

1774
The First Continental Congress meets in Philadelphia. Deborah Franklin dies of a stroke at age 66.

1775
Appointed to the Second Continental Congress. Elected postmaster general of the colonies. Invents odometer.

1776
Benjamin Franklin signs the Declaration of Independence, goes to France as a diplomat.

1783
Signs peace treaty with Britain.

1784
Invents bifocals.

1787
Signs the U.S. Constitution.

1789
Becomes president of the Society for Promoting the Abolition of Slavery.

April 17, 1790
Benjamin Franklin dies at age 84.

1790

A Man of Many Legacies

Hide not your talents, they for use were made.
What's a sun-dial in the shade?

What do libraries, streetlights, and fire stations have in common? What about bifocal glasses? Sayings like "haste makes waste"? The answer can be found on the U.S. $100 bill: Benjamin Franklin.

Franklin and his family lived in America when it was made up of thirteen colonies, ruled by the British king and run by his army. Ben's family was poor, but they knew that this little boy—so smart and curious about how things worked—could become something. His family was wrong—he became *many* things, including author, inventor, scientist, diplomat, community leader, and philosopher. His signature is on the Declaration of Independence. By the time Benjamin Franklin died, his work, inventions, and discoveries had touched the lives of every person in the new United States of America. Many of his achievements still touch lives around the world more than two hundred years later.

CHAPTER 1

The Roots of Greatness

It was a pleasure to me to see good workmen handle their tools. . . . [From them I learned to] be able to do little jobs myself in my house . . . and to construct little machines for my experiments.

If you were a family's youngest son in the 1700s, your parents probably would not have had enough money to send you to school or find you an apprenticeship. Parents usually helped their sons from the oldest down to the youngest. Any money a family had saved for its children had already been spent on the older boys by the time it was the youngest's turn. Daughters were taught at home, if

Benjamin Franklin was part of a very large family. He was one of seventeen children, which was unusual even by the standards of colonial times. This undated engraving shows how family life during that era centered around the kitchen.

they were taught at all. Benjamin was the youngest boy of Josiah Franklin's seventeen children.

Born in Boston, Massachusetts, on January 17, 1706, Benjamin did have something that could be thought of as his inheritance: a family history of independence. Josiah Franklin could trace his roots to 1540 in Ecton, England. Many members of the family had moved from the village to look for work. Some of them also did not agree with the country's powerful church and government officials. These two problems led many people to leave England for America, including Josiah, who sailed for Boston in 1683.

Josiah Franklin sailed from Ecton, England, in 1683 to find a better life in America. He probably sailed on a ship like the *Resolution*, shown in this painting, c. 1670.

Josiah was excited to live in a place where he could earn two to three times as much as he had in England. The cost of food, clothing, and shelter was not as high, either. Once in America, though, Josiah faced a big problem. In England, he had worked for his older brother to learn how to beautifully dye materials. However, Massachusetts, where the Franklins settled, was home to many **Puritans**. Most Puritans disapproved of people wearing bright colors or fancy clothes, so Josiah had to look for another kind of work.

He decided to become a tallow chandler, someone who made animal fat into soaps and candles. There were fewer men in this business because the hot and smelly job was so bad. Women happily bought his goods instead of making them at home. Josiah would not become rich as a chandler, but he would always have work.

Growing Up in Boston

Josiah's first wife, Anne, died sixteen years before Benjamin was born. Josiah had met Abiah, Ben's mother, at church, not long after Anne's death. Their small home on the corner of Milk and High Streets was filled with ten children besides Benjamin. They shared space with Josiah's candle-and soap-making equipment.

Benjamin would have had even more brothers and sisters, but four of them died very young. These early deaths were not unusual. At the time, there were no hospitals and few good doctors. One out of every four babies born in Boston died before it was a week old. However, in the busy Franklin home, life was more hectic than in most. One son, Ebenezer, slipped away from his family and drowned in a tub of soapsuds when he was sixteen months old.

For most children, growing up in this setting was hard at best. However, Benjamin Franklin was not like most children. Even early on, there were signs that he was special: Josiah and Abiah's little boy learned to read all by himself.

When Josiah decided that Benjamin would go to Harvard University someday, it was not just the boy's bright mind that his father considered. It was Josiah's attempt to **tithe** to the Puritan church his tenth son instead of one-tenth of his income. People could do one or the other in the 1700s. If they were poor, but had a lot of children, they could have their tenth son work for their church.

Benjamin, Josiah thought, would become a minister, and

Ben's father, Josiah Franklin, became a candle and soap maker, which was not the most pleasant work to undertake.

Harvard was where ministers trained. Ben's father sent him to Boston Latin School, so that he would later be ready for Harvard. Ben quickly rose to the top of the class and was allowed to skip ahead a grade, but his father took him out of the school after just a year. Josiah had decided that his youngest son—cocky and not at all religious—simply was not fit for a life of serving the church. If his son was not going to give himself to God, Josiah was not going to give his hard-earned money to an education that his son would not need.

Even though Franklin never had the opportunity to attend Harvard, he was eventually presented with this honorary master of arts degree in 1753 and wrote, "without studying at any college, I came to partake of their honours."

Benjamin was sent two blocks away to a regular school that taught writing and mathematics. He did very well in writing but failed at mathematics. Again, after one year, Ben's father pulled him from school. Josiah was again worried about money. So, at the age of ten, Ben's formal education was at an end.

Ben was now the last son still at home. Although Ben no longer went to school, Josiah made learning at home important. He knew that his sons would probably work as tradesmen. However, he still wanted them to have sharp, strong minds even if they were printers or soap makers. Books and stirring talks filled the little house, which gave many chances for a child with an eager mind to learn.

Josiah often invited well-spoken friends with strong opinions to join the Franklins at supper. He wanted to share their talks with his entire family. These guests were usually prominent men from Josiah's church or the community. Benjamin's love of arguing with interesting people began at his father's dinner table.

Young Ben Goes to Work

It seemed to Ben that his future might be full of steaming vats of animal fat, just like his father's. Ben found his days filled with the awful job of skimming dirt and scum from the boiling pots of fat. Other tasks he had were just as boring. He cut wicks for candles and ran errands for his father. He could not see himself spending his life this way. Instead, he wanted to try his hand at his great love, the sea.

Josiah would not hear of it. One of his older sons, Josiah Jr., had run off and drowned at sea. He would not let Benjamin risk the same fate. So, Josiah took Benjamin to visit various tradesmen at work in their shops, hoping to find practical work that would interest the boy.

Watching blacksmiths, bricklayers, and other craftsmen at work had a lasting effect on Benjamin. "It was," he would one

Franklin's Family

Josiah's Children with Anne Child
1. Elizabeth (1678–1759)
2. Samuel (1681–1720)
3. Hannah (1683–1723)
4. Josiah (1685–1715)
5. Anne (1687–1729)
6. Joseph I (Feb. 6–11, 1688)
7. Joseph II (June 30–July 15, 1689)

Josiah's Children with Abiah Folger
8. John (1690–1756)
9. Peter (1692–1766)
10. Mary (1694–1731)
11. James (1697–1735)
12. Sarah (1699–1731)
13. Ebenezer (1701–1703)
14. Thomas (1703–1706)
15. Benjamin (1706–1790)
16. Lydia (1708–1758)
17. Jane (1712–1794)

The woman in this portrait is believed to be Abiah Franklin, the second wife of Josiah and the mother of Ben Franklin.

day recall, "a pleasure to me to see good workmen handle their tools." He also said that he learned enough from these men to " . . . be able to do little jobs myself in my house . . . and to construct little machines for my experiments."

Learning how to make knives from his cousin was another job Benjamin did not want. Josiah looked for another way his son could earn a living. Benjamin's twenty-one-year-old brother James had just come home from London, where he had learned to be a printer. Josiah hoped that printing might be interesting enough to keep Benjamin from running off to sea.

Josiah hoped that printing might be interesting enough to keep Benjamin from running off to sea.

Printing seemed like the best possibility. Although he had only two years of formal education, twelve-year-old Benjamin liked nothing better than to read. From the time he first began to earn money, he would save up to buy new books. When he finished reading one, he sold it and bought another.

Josiah and James had Benjamin sign **indenture** papers that promised he would be an apprentice in his brother's new printing business until he, too, was twenty-one. Benjamin now had a contract that said he would work only for his brother for nine years. He would not stay that long with James, but Ben would have a long-lasting legacy as a printer.

Throughout his life, Ben Franklin was an avid reader. Young Ben is shown reading by candlelight in this 1852 engraving.

An Inventor Emerges

While swimming with friends in the Charles River, young Benjamin did more than splash around and dunk his friends. One day, he noticed that the size of someone's hands helped him to move faster through the water, which made him try to think of a way to make his hands bigger. His first design was made of two oval, wooden boards with holes for his thumbs. When he held one on each hand, he could swim faster and not get tired as quickly. (Later in life, he would improve this design and come up with swim fins similar to the kind used by divers today.)

His other early invention, which was part water-skiing, part paragliding, came from an idea about his kite. Lying on his back in a lake, he held the stick of the kite and let the wind blow him across the water. The ride gave him "the greatest pleasure imaginable."

Ben's ingenuity gave him the idea to create "fins" for the body, which would help a person swim faster and with greater ease. Today, fins for the feet are commonly used by swimmers of all ages.

CHAPTER 2

Ben Learns His Trade

Either write something worth reading or do something worth writing.

Twelve-year-old Benjamin enjoyed learning his new trade. Setting type and helping with different jobs at James's print shop did not take much effort. The print shop gave Benjamin contact with many good books as soon as they were printed, and he spent much of his free time reading whatever he could. He began to save his food money by eating only a vegetarian diet, because it was cheaper to eat meals without meat. He bought more books with the money he saved.

He also found new books through the friend of a friend. A boy who worked at the bookseller's shop passed on many books to Ben by taking books from the shop without permission and giving them to Ben. Ben then read through the night and made sure the books were given back early the next morning so they would not be missed. This went on until Ben met a regular customer at his brother's print shop

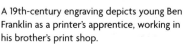

A 19th-century engraving depicts young Ben Franklin as a printer's apprentice, working in his brother's print shop.

named Matthew Adams. Adams let young Ben Franklin borrow any book he wanted to read from his large family library. These books included some exciting poems, which is how Benjamin discovered and started writing poetry.

When James noticed that his brother was writing short poems, he asked him to create two poems to be specially printed on single sheets of paper. It was not a love of poetry that moved James; it was money. He had a steady contract to print the *Boston Gazette*, but wanted more. He had seen printers in London produce sheets of poetry about current events and sell them on the streets for a nice profit. If his brother so loved the printed word, why not see if he could write something to add to James's earnings?

Ben's older brother James Franklin was the first printer for the *Boston Gazette*. A 1721 issue of the newspaper is shown here.

Had he been the sort to discourage easily, poetry could have been Benjamin Franklin's undoing. He wrote the requested pieces, peddled them around town, and found that one of them sold quite well. It was a thrill for the beginning writer—a thrill that his father quickly squashed. Poets, he informed his son, usually ended up in the poorhouse—especially when they were as bad at it as Ben was. "So I escaped being a poet, most probably a very bad one," Benjamin would later agree, even calling his poems "wretched." However, he was closing in on his future. **Prose**, not poetry, would make him a household name.

Ben was not a very good writer at first, and knew it, so he made up games to help himself improve. One tool he used was to write a letter to a friend with whom he had a heated debate. When the friend wrote back, Benjamin saw how the boy's better writing made his thoughts look stronger than they really were. The boys kept their arguments going in their letters, and Ben's writing grew better and better using this exercise.

Another self-help game Benjamin invented was to read and reread a book he found interesting. He would then try to rewrite it and make it better. He would compare his work to the original after he was done. As Ben kept practicing, his writing improved quite a bit. He was very pleased with himself when he could make a book better than it was when he first read it.

Sibling Rivalry

As Benjamin's writing improved, his relationship with his brother got worse. James was jealous of his young brother's new talent. He went out of his way to insult Ben and often beat him.

The anger that slowly built in Benjamin would stay with him for most of his life. Much later, Benjamin would say that his brother's unfair treatment made Ben dislike people who

This undated illustration shows Ben selling his poetry around town.

James was usually at odds with Ben and often treated him badly. This 1852 engraving shows James about to wallop his young brother.

used their positions of power to hurt others. For now, though, James was in charge, so Ben learned ways to handle him.

Ben's best way of getting back at his older brother came in 1721. James began to publish his own newspaper, the *New England Courant*. The paper was full of free-thinking opinions and jests. It was America's first independent newspaper and was not afraid to poke fun at life and the government.

James's friends often wrote pieces for the *Courant*. They loved to talk about the praise they received from readers. Benjamin wanted townspeople to talk about his writing, too, but he knew that James would tear up anything he wrote. To get around James, Ben wrote essays secretly, using made-up pen names. Some of those names were Harry Meanwell, Anthony Afterwit, Alice Addertongue, and Richard Saunders. These authors would slip "their" pieces under the shop door after James left for the evening.

At 16 years of age, Ben wrote essays for the *Courant* under various pen names, including "Mrs. Silence Dogood."

People all over Boston talked about the essays, which they thought were funny and interesting. Usually, newspapers were full of reports from England about government, notices of ships coming and going from port, and other ordinary things, but the compositions in the *New England Courant* made people laugh and want to read more.

To get around James, Ben wrote essays secretly, using made-up pen names.

The teenaged Ben listened with glee as James's friends tried to guess whom the writer might be. They suggested only the names of the smartest and most skilled men in the city.

James then printed fourteen witty essays on life in Massachusetts by "Mrs. Silence Dogood," really written by sixteen-year-old Benjamin Franklin. He had tricked his brother into printing his essays, which had the paper's readers wondering who the writer was. Could it really be an old woman from the country? However, Mrs. Dogood's amusing stories

The Life of an Apprentice

Apprenticeships were formal contracts that traded a boy's hard labor for a skilled craftsman's training. A master made all the rules and expected the apprentice to obey. Parents often loaned out their sons in such deals. Very few daughters became apprentices—their training was at home.

The average length of this kind of contract was seven years. Part of this contract included that the master had to provide for the young man's care and education. During the seven-year contract, many boys were often treated badly and were not allowed to return home at all. Many just ran away.

An apprentice was not paid until his contract was over, when the craftsman was expected to send off the boy with "freedom dues" of clothing, money, and tools to help him start his own business.

During colonial times, young boys were often loaned out to craftsmen, who would train their young apprentices. This 18th-century engraving shows a bricklayer being helped by his apprentice.

quickly came to an end. James had picked up on clues in the composition and began to suspect the true writer. Benjamin told readers his real name in Mrs. Dogood's final story, which did not make James happy.

Not everyone was a fan of the stories and news printed in the *New England Courant*, though. From the start, the rebel *Courant* made it a point to poke fun at the colony's government officials. Most newspapers of the time printed only news about officials that the officials themselves would like. In 1722, James was so good at making officials angry with his articles that he was thrown in jail for a month. Later, he did the same thing again. Officials gave him the choice of a longer jail term or giving up his job as publisher of the *Courant*. James took the second choice.

James's problems were a lucky break for Benjamin. However, it would start a new fight between the brothers, one that would

In a move to save his brother James from jail, Ben was named publisher of the *Courant* and actually began running the newspaper.

ruin the Franklin brothers' relationship for the rest of their lives.

James and Josiah came up with a way to get around the order banning James as publisher of the newspaper. They realized that they could keep the paper going if Ben appeared to take over. So, they put his name on the paper's **masthead** instead of James's and drew up fake papers that released Ben from the rest of his indenture. James never really intended for Ben to take over—he just wanted it to look that way.

In light of the new arrangement, Benjamin refused to honor his original apprenticeship. He knew that James could not afford to call attention to the trick. Benjamin Franklin ran the *Courant* as he saw fit, while James seethed in the background.

Bidding Boston Good-bye

The next fight that the brothers had led a now bolder Benjamin to quit his brother's shop. He thought there must be other printers in town who would want his help. He also suspected that other printers would not beat him, as James continued to do.

Ben's walkout might have worked if James had not quickly talked to all the other printers in Boston before Ben did. He made sure Benjamin was blacklisted from every other print shop in the city, which meant that no other printer would hire Ben. The older brother wanted Ben to stay on and run his shop in secret.

Benjamin saw only one choice—he had to run away. He sold some of his books to pay his passage on a ship sailing for New York, and he had a friend buy his ticket in secret, in case James tried to stop him. On September 25, 1723, Boston faded out of view for Benjamin Franklin, age seventeen, but his future was not to be in New York.

port. From there, they were shipped to the West Indies and London. London then sent back manufactured goods. Many traders in Philadelphia became rich and lived well.

What Benjamin Franklin would find he liked the most about Philadelphia was that the city's peace-loving Quakers welcomed all religions. Back in Boston, Puritan leaders were less friendly to people of other beliefs. Philadelphia better suited Ben's feelings about religion.

The thrill of those first few minutes in Philadelphia would stay in Franklin's memory forever. As an old man, looking back at the dirty, tired young Ben would make him laugh.

At the moment, however, he was a mess. He was dressed in

Ben found the Quakers of Philadelphia to be a welcoming group.
This 19th-century engraving shows a Quaker meeting in Philadelphia.

Pressing Matters

Printing may have been thought of as one of the best trades in the 1700s, but it was not exciting or easy work. Men who became printers had to be strong or have strong help. The work was hard on a man's back as well as on his eyes. Shops were not well lit, the poor-quality ink smeared on the worn-down type, and each page of a book or newspaper had to be printed one at a time.

The first press was invented in the 1440s, in Germany. The presses themselves were made of wood, but many printers used metal type. (Iron presses would not appear until the early 1800s.) Men had to press the ink onto the paper by pushing hard on levers and screws. Each letter of type was pulled from a set of alphabet blocks and laid into place upside down, one at a time, word by word—then put back in their place after a page was printed.

Today's students learn to write using *uppercase* and *lowercase* letters. These terms came from the cases, or boxes, used by early printers to organize their type. The capital letters were in an "upper" case, and the small letters were in a "lower" case. When a worker needed to capitalize a word, he took a capital letter from the box on top. Small letters were picked up from the box on the bottom.

Well into the 20th century, type was still being set by hand using individual letters that were stored in wooden cases.
This photo shows a newspaper typesetter in 1950.

shabby work clothes, and his pockets were stuffed with extra shirts and stockings. He was also very hungry. With the few coins in his pocket making up all his money, he paid for his final ship ride and then bought three huge "puffy rolls," a kind of bread he'd never seen before. With a roll tucked under each arm and one crammed into his mouth, he wandered up Market Street to Fourth Street.

Standing in the doorway of one of the houses was a young woman. She thought that he made a "most awkward ridiculous appearance." Deborah Read would remember her first look at Benjamin Franklin for the rest of her life.

This 19th-century engraving depicts Benjamin as a scruffy and hungry young man walking down a street of Philadelphia and passing by a young lady, who would eventually become his wife.

Hired as a Printer

After a few days of rest and food, Ben found Andrew Bradford, owner of the *American Weekly Mercury*. Andrew gave Ben breakfast and a temporary room, but he did not give him a job, because he had just hired someone else.

Benjamin's luck was a little better when he went to Bradford's competitor, Samuel Keimer. Keimer's shop and equipment were both poor. With his experience and mechanically inclined mind, Benjamin had no trouble convincing Keimer that he would be a useful employee. With Ben's help, Keimer's press and letter fonts were working better in just a few days. Ben had a job.

Both Bradford and Keimer seemed to Benjamin to be the wrong people for the printing trade. Keimer was intelligent and always happy to debate with Franklin, but was clumsy with the printing press. Bradford, the other printer, could not even read well! However, any problems Ben had with these men were minor. Wonderful opportunities were coming together for him in this busy city.

By working hard and being careful with his money, he saw his savings start to grow. This was a first for Ben. He became friendly

This 19th-century engraving shows young Franklin working as a printer in Philadelphia. Soon after arriving in Philadelphia, Benjamin went to work for printer Samuel Keimer.

with a group of young tradesmen who also loved to read, and spent many interesting evenings talking with them.

Having his employee live with his rival, Bradford, was not what Keimer wanted. Keimer's landlord had a room for rent in his own home, so Ben was sent there. The landlord was none other than John Read, whose house Benjamin had passed in his first moments off the dock—the one where the young girl had stood staring in amusement at him.

This time, when Ben actually met the young girl, whose name was Miss Deborah Read, he was dressed in his better clothes (they had since been shipped to him in a trunk). After a while, he found that he had "a great respect and affection for

This 1852 engraving shows Benjamin courting Miss Deborah Read.

her," and believed that she felt the same. They began a slow and careful courtship.

If Deborah had been the sort of girl who hoped for a wonderful romance and a quick wedding, she would have been very disappointed. Benjamin Franklin was a man with plans, and those plans were about to lead him away from her.

A Capital Idea

Soon Benjamin realized he had enough training, experience, and talent to open a printing shop of his own. What he did not have was enough money.

Luck led him closer to his dream. Ben had written a letter to his brother-in-law, telling him how very much he liked Philadelphia. Ben's relative thought that Sir William Keith, the governor of Pennsylvania, might enjoy reading the letter. Keith did, and was also very impressed by Ben's writing. Keith gave not only praise to Benjamin, but was willing to help him start his own shop. Benjamin Franklin should become a printer of whom the city could be proud. The governor would make sure there was plenty of government printing work for Franklin. If Benjamin could find the money to start the business, then Keith would help keep it going.

That "if," Benjamin told Keith, was a "cannot."

Keith was not upset by Franklin's lack of money. He continued for weeks afterward to have dinner with his young (and surprised) friend. Finally, he said that Benjamin should sail back to Boston to visit his family and ask his father for the needed money. To help Benjamin ask for the loan, Keith wrote a letter to Josiah about Benjamin's talent and promise.

A portrait of Sir William Keith, who served as governor of Pennsylvania. Impressed with Franklin, Governor Keith encouraged Ben to open up his own print shop and promised to help young Franklin.

In all the time he was in Philadelphia, Ben had not written to let his family know he was alive and well. Now, he was going back to Boston to ask his father for help.

Not So Fast

Josiah Franklin was thrilled to see his son again. As Ben had hoped, the governor's letter about Benjamin's talents impressed his father. The senior Mr. Franklin agreed that Benjamin could be a great success—just not quite yet.

Josiah did not feel sure that Benjamin could be trusted with the family's hard-earned money. At only eighteen, Ben had a lot to learn about life and his trade. Josiah thought he would feel better about giving Ben money once the boy had three more years of growing up. Go back to Philadelphia, Josiah said, and keep saving money. If Benjamin could earn enough to come close to the amount needed, Josiah would supply the rest. It was the best deal Benjamin was able to make.

Josiah had been pleased to see how well his youngest son was doing on his own, but James was a different story altogether. When Benjamin stopped by James's shop to see him, the young brother was wearing fine clothing and had a fancy pocket watch. His pockets jangled with plenty of coins, too. After a long stare, James turned his back on Benjamin and kept on working. Neither brother had said a word.

Ben Sets Sail for Britain

Back in Philadelphia, Governor Keith was sorry that Josiah refused to help his youngest son. He still wanted to see Benjamin open a print shop, though. Keith told Benjamin to sail to London and buy the presses and supplies he needed. As an agent of Great Britain, Keith would sign the official papers that promised payment for both the trip and machines.

Happy to do as Keith said, Benjamin broke the news to Deborah. When the sailing ship *Annis* left in a few months for its once-a-year trip to Britain, he would be on it. Benjamin promised they could resume their friendship when he returned.

Keith told Benjamin to sail to London and buy the presses and supplies he needed.

He would not exactly keep his word to Deborah. Neither would Governor Keith keep his promises to Ben.

This sailing trip was very different from Ben's last one. He was much more comfortable, and was joined on the ship by his best friend, a young Philadelphia poet named James Ralph.

An engraving, c. 1800, shows Governor Keith with a Colonel French visiting Ben in a print shop. Franklin later said of Governor Keith, "[He] wished to please everybody; and, having little to give, he gave expectations."

However, Benjamin was shocked to find that there were no letters of credit waiting for him in London. Governor Keith had not sent along the payment for the trip and Ben's new presses.

Thomas Denham, a kind Quaker, was also sailing on the *Annis*. He took a liking to Ben and told him about Governor Keith's well-known character. Keith was not a wicked man, but suffered from delusions of grandeur, which means that he wanted more money and influence than he actually had, so he *acted* as if he had wealth and power, when he really had neither. By the time the ship docked in London on December 24, 1724, Ben owed for the trip there, had no money for the trip home, and, had nowhere to go. Fortunately, young Ben Franklin did not discourage easily. He would find a way to succeed.

CHAPTER 4

Building Bridges in London

The way to wealth depends on just two words, industry and frugality.

If Benjamin Franklin was going to be stranded anywhere, the booming city of London was a good place for it. A printer with skill and talent was rare and much needed. Franklin was quickly hired at a famous printing house, Samuel Palmer's, where he would work for the next year.

In the 1700s, a single man living in a rented room and

Upon arriving in London, Franklin took advantage of all that the city had to offer. This 19th-century engraving of London, c. 1710, depicts a scene that Ben might have observed as he walked near the streets of St. James's Palace.

While living in London, Ben gave little thought to Deborah Read in Philadelphia. Instead, he enjoyed his new friends and the social life that London had to offer. An example of that carefree lifestyle is depicted in this 18th-century print of crowds enjoying the Greenwich Fair near London.

earning a good salary should have been able to save most of his money, at least enough for a few trips across the Atlantic Ocean. Ben, however, spent every penny he earned as soon as he got it. London had many more interesting things to see than Philadelphia, and Benjamin Franklin wanted to see all of them. He spent most of his evenings with his friend James Ralph. James was always broke and asking Ben for money, so Ben ended up paying for James's dinners and fun, too.

During his entire year in England, Ben wrote just one short and unfriendly letter to Deborah Read in Philadelphia. Instead of writing to Deborah, Ben would go out. Sometimes, he would go to plays. Other times, he would join in debate with friends, or meet with other poets and writers. He met new and exciting people, and did not seem to miss Deborah at all.

Life was not so good for Deborah Read. She understood clearly from Ben's one brief, cold letter to her that he was in no hurry to return. Instead of waiting for him, she married a sweet-talking man named John Rogers. This marriage turned out so badly that Deborah might have been better off waiting to see if Benjamin's feelings would change. Rogers, it turned out, could not hold a steady job, and owed money to lots of people. Some people were also whispering that he had another wife, in England. Deborah left him and moved in with her widowed mother. John Rogers stole a slave and ran away to the West Indies. The people he owed money were left unpaid.

Deborah Read, shown in this 18th-century portrait, felt rejected by Ben's less than enthusiastic letter and married another man, who deserted her soon after they were married.

Soon after, a rumor spread that he had died on the islands, but no one knew for sure. Deborah was trapped. Without proof that she was a widow, the law would not allow her to marry another man.

Focusing on His Career

However grand life was for Franklin, he knew that he had to return to America sometime, but knew that he would need money to do so. Losing James Ralph as a friend made saving money easier. A horrible fight they had over Ralph's girlfriend ended their friendship forever. Ben knew he would never get back the money he had loaned James, but he thought it was well spent just to be rid of him.

Franklin began to put all his energy into his career. One of the boldest things he did was to write, print, and distribute a pamphlet about his religious views. He realized, too late, that the pamphlet was awful and full of ideas that were not well thought out. However, two important things came of this event.

First, it made people take note of him. Men of the upper classes, as well as those with money, invited him for drinks and debate. Second, even though the pamphlet was not as good as Ben had hoped, it marked the beginning of Ben's trademark style of writing and thinking about important matters. His writing would be based on practical, common sense, and he presented ideas that people could use to make both their daily lives and their government better.

Benjamin Franklin, the thinker, may have gotten off to a shaky start, but Ben the saver did better. He rented a cheaper room and watched how much money he spent on eating and drinking. Some nights, he went

Franklin began to put all his energy into his career.

back to reading his favorite books instead of going out. He even got a higher-paying job with the printer John Watts, even though his job had worked out well at Palmer's.

A little later, the man he met on his voyage to London,

At one point, Benjamin went to work for London printer John Watts. This 1858 engraving shows Franklin in Watts's printing office.

Quaker merchant Thomas Denham, talked him into returning home. Denham's plan was for them to open a store together. Benjamin would work for him for a year at a fifty-pound salary (about $8,000 in today's money), less than he made in London. In return, Denham would pay for Ben's trip home. This plan sounded good to Ben because in America, merchants held higher status than printers. Benjamin and Denham boarded the ship to return home in July 1726.

Franklin could look back on his year and a half in London and have reason to be proud. He had accomplished a lot for a twenty-year-old. However, it was not in his nature to look back. Ben was always thinking about tomorrow.

He passed the time on the return trip by studying the sea around him, and by working on one of his biggest projects yet: He made a list he called his "Plan for Future Conduct," which he would be prouder of than just about anything he would later write. In it, he stated goals for making himself a better person, as

Together with his Quaker friend Thomas Denham, Ben headed back to America in 1726, where they planned to open up a store. There were many kinds of shops during that era; this tinware shop was just one type of store during colonial times.

well as his plans for how to reach these goals:

> *To live as cheaply as possible until he paid off his debts . . .*
>
> *To always tell the truth and keep his promises . . .*
>
> *To stick to hard work and patience . . .*
>
> *To speak ill of no man whatever.*

As he sailed toward America, he must have thought about all he had learned in London, and how he might use that knowledge when he reached Philadelphia.

Waves of Observations

Each time he sailed the Atlantic, Ben paid attention to the sea all around him. As a result, he was able to come up with some important ideas in natural science. His first trip, however, was mostly spent testing and thinking. He timed the eclipse of the moon because he knew that it somehow related to charting the ship's location. He studied the sky and saw that a full moon during a light rain could make a rainbow at night. He also made one funny mistake: When he pulled a clump of seaweed from the water and saw little crabs clinging to it, he thought the seaweed was *making* the crabs, almost as though the crabs were babies born from the seaweed. He pulled out another batch of seaweed and watched it closely. It produced nothing. His experiment showed him he was wrong, but his mistakes did not discourage him.

On his voyage back to America, Franklin observed a rainbow at night during a full moon and light rain. This modern photo taken in New Mexico captures the same type of natural phenomenon.

CHAPTER 5

Philadelphia, a Perfect Fit

This country man's five shillings…gave me more pleasure than any crown I have since earned.

Back on the streets of Philadelphia, Benjamin Franklin looked over all that had changed during his eighteen months in London. One thing that did not surprise him was that William Keith was no longer governor. When Benjamin passed him on the street, Keith did not say a word. In fact, Keith was so ashamed that he would not even look at Ben.

Keith could not know that Franklin had him to thank for a firm push toward his future greatness—London had taught Benjamin just how much he could accomplish. Soon, twenty-one-year-old Benjamin Franklin went to work in Thomas Denham's clothing and hardware store.

London had taught Benjamin just how much he could accomplish.

He quickly learned what it took to do well as a tradesman. Benjamin might have opened his own store in time, because he liked the work and was very good at it. However, Denham died suddenly a few months after Franklin started working for him.

After Denham's death, lawyers handling his property took over the store, and Ben was out of a job once again. Soon, he was back working for Samuel Keimer (the clumsy printer).

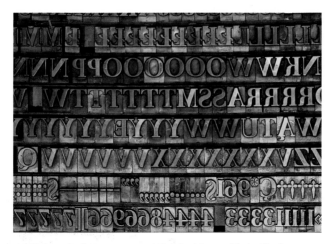

Franklin was the first to use strong and durable metal letter blocks, instead of wood, for the printing press. The metal type in this photograph is backwards as it would have been arranged at an actual printing press.

Keimer offered Franklin a very high salary, and Ben soon found out why. A number of journeyman printers worked in the shop. It was Keimer's plan to have Ben train them until they were good at their jobs. Then, he thought, Ben could be fired!

Franklin figured out Keimer's scheme, but that did not stop him from working hard and thinking of ways to improve the shop. He used Keimer's old wooden type letters to make new ones from lead molds. He was the first person in America to make metal type for a printing press. To save the shop money, he even made his own ink instead of buying it.

Ben also created a special press to print money for the New Jersey colony. In the 1700s, colonies could give the job of printing their money to any printer they chose. There was no government agency that printed all of the money for the colonies. Ben's efforts helped Keimer get the contract to print New Jersey's money.

Ben continued to make improvements and was a better businessman than Keimer. One of Keimer's journeymen, Hugh

It was a common sight in Philadelphia to see Franklin hauling rolls of paper to his print shop.

borrowed money and bought out the other half of the business. Hugh Meredith was easy to like but hard to work with. Ben figured that, because he was doing all the work, he should own the business. At only twenty-four years old, Ben did. He achieved all of this in less than two years.

Ben was quickly putting down roots in Philadelphia. With his business doing well, it was time for him to branch out beyond his print shop, time to begin some of the many self-improvement and community projects that had been tugging at him. Marriage was at the top of his list of self-improvements. People married young in colonial days. Ben felt it did not look right for a man of twenty-four not to have a wife.

He met many women, but he could not find one with a big enough dowry (the money a family gave to a woman's new husband) to fit his goals. In the end, he went back to Deborah Read Rogers. With her first husband's whereabouts a mystery, Deborah and Benjamin could not have a real wedding. They moved in together as common-law husband and wife in 1730, which was not an unusual way for people to marry in the colonies.

Deborah was at last married to Benjamin Franklin—one of the city's most up-and-coming men. Ben asked Deborah to

Plagued By Pleurisy

During the time when Ben was starting to do well in his business in the late 1720s, he developed a health problem. He came down with a disease called pleurisy, which is usually caused by a lung infection.

Franklin felt like his lungs were two pieces of sandpaper rubbing together with every breath. It also made him feel as though he was not getting enough oxygen. Pleurisy "very nearly carried me off," Franklin recalled in a bit of a dramatic manner. "I suffered a good deal, gave up the point in my own mind, and was rather disappointed when I found myself recovering." He feared having the sickness return, and unfortunately it would for the rest of his life.

become the mother of his little son William, whom he had fathered with another woman. Ben's new wife did not give Benjamin the help in society that he had hoped for, and they did not love each other deeply. In a time when families were very large, they only had two children, perhaps because they were not very close. Deborah did, however, make Ben's life much more comfortable.

Debby, as Ben called her, was very afraid of traveling and never went with Ben on any of his journeys. Some say she never even left Philadelphia. When she had a stroke in 1774, Benjamin was living in Europe. She died without having seen her husband in fifteen years.

Deborah Franklin tried to be a good wife to Benjamin and helped him in every way possible. This 1852 engraving shows Mrs. Franklin working in his printing office.

To Lead a Good and Honest Life

Ben Franklin mixed his personal standards with what he learned from the many books he read. In 1784, Franklin came up with a list of qualities he felt a person must have to lead a good and honest life. After reading them, a friend pointed out that Benjamin should include one that would help to keep his huge ego under control—humility.

Temperance. Do not eat or drink too much.

Silence. If you cannot say anything good, do not say anything at all.

Order. Have a place for everything. Set a time for every activity.

Resolution. No matter what, do what you have to do.

Frugality. Waste nothing.

Industry. Always be doing something useful. Do not waste time.

Sincerity. Do not lie. Think the best of people.

Justice. Do right by people. Give credit where it is due.

Moderation. Keep away from extremes.

Cleanliness. Keep your body, clothing, and house clean.

Tranquility. Do not let little things bother you, especially things that are accidental or could not be stopped.

Each day of the week, Franklin tried his best to be perfect in one of the areas he listed. "I wished to live without committing any fault at any time," he confessed. He made a note of every time he slipped up and failed to meet his goal. But he claimed that he was a better and happier man for at least having tried.

The club had members of different religions, which was an important part of life in colonial times. In their talks, members often argued about their different beliefs. Benjamin Franklin's views on the subject were brought out, too. He did not often go to church, but did pay yearly dues to a Presbyterian church that had "rightly conducted" services.

He did not agree with many of the common beliefs of his day. However, he agreed that religion was important because it sometimes helped people to behave honestly and kindly. Nothing mattered more to Ben than trying to be a good man. He also believed in doing good for others. These ideas were at the heart of his belief in God and his feelings about citizenship.

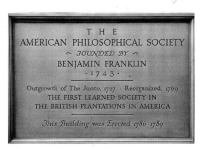

The Junto Club eventually grew into the American Philosophical Society in 1743. The plaque reminds visitors that the APS is an "Outgrowth of The Junto 1727."

Over time the Junto grew large enough to move its meetings from a public room to a rented, private room. Within a few years, the club was so much fun and so useful to its members that new branches were formed. For many years, Junto meetings would be one of Franklin's favorite and most important works. Some of Benjamin Franklin's greatest ideas got their start in the Junto.

The American Philosophical Society

Ben Franklin's work took him throughout the colonies, so he was able to learn more about other people and their ideas than most Americans of the time. With the success of the Junto club, Franklin thought it would be a good idea to start a similar type of club that covered all the colonies. So, in 1743 he organized the American Philosophical Society (APS). This group brought together some of the leading thinkers in science, history, the arts, and politics. The members discussed new ideas and explored new discoveries. Franklin asked that, as much as possible, the work of the APS be of use to American citizens.

The seal of the American Philosophical Society, with its Latin phrase "Nullo Discrimine," suggests a society "Without Discrimination."

More than sixty years later, APS of Philadelphia has more than nine hundred members. It still does research projects, and prints research papers and books. The society also continues to honor discoveries that improve people's lives.

For the Love of Reading

During the first half of the eighteenth century, reading for pleasure was not a common practice. Books were expensive— partly because they came all the way from England. Ben Franklin wanted to give all Philadelphians a chance to read more, but he felt there were no good bookstores south of Boston. He was sure a city lending library would be a good idea.

In 1731, as an offshoot of the Junto club, Franklin started the Library Company of Philadelphia. Junto members had to pay a starting fee of forty shillings ($320 in today's money), and yearly dues of ten shillings ($80), which was used to buy new books. Members went to the library once a week to borrow books that they wanted to read. Anyone who did not return books had to pay a large fine, so people were generally good about bringing books back on time. Twenty-seven-year-old Ben liked to see how much people enjoyed the library, which soon became worthy of the slogan he chose for it: "To pour forth benefits for the common good is divine."

The idea spread throughout Pennsylvania. New libraries were even able to get start-up money from sponsors instead of charging membership fees. "Reading became fashionable." Franklin boasted about how well the libraries worked, "Our people…were observed by strangers to be better instructed and more intelligent than people of the same rank generally are in other countries." The Library Company is still open today. Its shelves hold over 500,000 books!

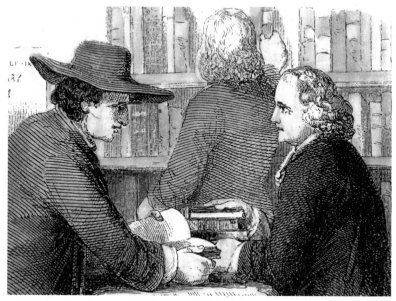

In this 19th-century engraving, Franklin is seen in the Library Company of Philadelphia, the first lending library in America.

Arriving at a Fair Tax

During the Junto years, Philadelphia families were protected at night by a City Watch patrol, an early police force, made up of men from different neighborhoods. They asked that local men take turns going on patrol with them. Anyone who did not want to help could pay six shillings ($48) per year to get out of the work. Most citizens wanted to be protected, but had no interest in patrolling. Many opted to pay the fee in order to avoid having to patrol, so the City Watch fund ended up with more money than it needed.

Franklin wrote a report criticizing the way in which the watch was run. He suggested that men be hired to patrol full time, and that the money to pay them should be raised through a tax. Franklin thought that people should pay that tax based on the worth of their homes and land, so that a poor widow would not pay as much as a wealthy merchant.

He read this paper to the Junto members. The club liked the ideas about fairer taxes and shared them with the other Junto

Franklin helped establish a fairer tax rate whereby wealthy owners of grand homes, like the one shown, paid a higher tax than poorer citizens who lived in smaller, modest homes. Depicted in this 19th-century engraving is the Robert Morris House in Philadelphia. It was home to President George Washington during his presidency.

groups in Philadelphia, but it took a long time for the city government to approve Ben's plans. Eventually, charging people a yearly tax based on the cost of their property was deemed acceptable. Many of Ben's club members, including himself, were now important leaders in Philadelphia. They were behind his plan and could put it to work. So, the colonies' first tax based on a person's ability to pay was adopted. It would become the model for how the future U.S. government would tax its citizens.

Fire Protection

One of the worst fires ever to happen in Philadelphia began on Fishbourne's Wharf in 1730. All the stores on the wharf and some houses across the street burned to the ground. In his newspaper, Benjamin Franklin scolded Philadelphians for not being ready to fight a fire. In Boston, he had seen that fire engines and men with buckets working together could stop a fire soon after it started. Franklin continued to write about the problem in his newspaper, as well as discussing it with his Junto group.

Writing as an "old citizen," he told readers of the *Gazette* that "an ounce of prevention is worth a pound of cure." He warned them to carry hot coals from one fireplace to another in a closed bucket, which would keep small, hot ashes from falling into cracks in the floor. He warned that the hot ashes could burn secretly in the wood floors and burst into flames in the middle of the night.

The model shown in this photograph is much like the hand-drawn fire engines of Franklin's day.

Otherwise, "you may be forced (as I once was) to leap out of your windows, and [risk] your necks to avoid being over-roasted."

Finally, city leaders ordered ladders and fire engines from London. Franklin wanted the city to copy the firefighting clubs that were popular in Boston, where each neighborhood had its own fire engine and a group of men in charge of putting out any fires that started in their area.

This painting c. 1850 by Charles Washington Wright shows Ben Franklin wearing a fire helmet from the Union Fire Company, which he helped organize in 1736.

When the Union Fire Company formed in 1736, thirty men agreed to join. They met each month to talk about new ways of keeping fires from starting and practiced how to stop any fire that broke out. The company was swamped with requests from men wanting to join. The Union members asked these men to form their own companies so that the whole city could be covered. Philadelphia soon saw the rise of the Hand-in-Hand, Fellowship, and Britannia fire companies and became thought of as one of the finest cities in the world for putting out fires. Near the end of his long life, Ben thought of these fire companies as one of his proudest successes.

Even though his plan for fire prevention worked very well, Ben Franklin knew more could be done for the city. In 1740, he helped start the very successful Philadelphia Contributorship, the country's first insurance company. For a fee, anyone could join. If a member had a fire at home or at work, the building would be fixed for free. A small metal plaque was tacked to the outside of a building to prove the fee was paid. Many of Philadelphia's historic homes still have their original Contributorship plaque.

An Early Environmentalist

There were many benefits to being a newspaper publisher. One was that Franklin could share issues that interested him with his readers. For example, businesses that killed animals and tanned their hides to make leather was a problem in Philadelphia. Although they provided food and leather goods, the companies would get rid of the animal remains by simply throwing them into rivers around the city. Franklin wrote newspaper articles asking the owners to stop in order to keep the water clean. He was one of the first Americans known to worry about the environment.

Benjamin used the power of his newspaper to fight for improved city conditions. This undated print shows newly paved streets in early Philadelphia.

He also used his newspaper to demand cleaner streets, suggesting that workers sweep the dirt roads every day. When this was done, Philadelphians saw that their clothes and the windows on their homes were cleaner, and the stores looked brighter. It was then easy for Franklin to rally them in favor of his next improvement: paving over the dirt streets of the city.

Dr. Thomas Bond

Thomas Bond was born in Philadelphia in 1712, but received his medical training in Europe. Together with Benjamin Franklin, they built the Pennsylvania Hospital, which was the first hospital in America. Dr. Bond often worked for free and was Deborah Read Franklin's doctor until she died.

The hospital became an important asset to the Continental army during the Revolutionary War by training doctors for wartime aid. It became a place where wounded men were cared for not just during the Revolutionary War, but during the Civil War (1861–1865), and the Spanish American War of 1898. Bond died in 1784 at the age of seventy-one and was known as the "Father of Clinical Medicine." Pennsylvania Hospital is still open today, and still provides quality medical care.

During the Revolutionary War, Dr. Thomas Bond helped to train doctors for the Continental army and is known as the "Father of Clinical Medicine."

Together with Thomas Bond, Benjamin Franklin helped build the first hospital in America—the Pennsylvania Hospital—which opened in 1752 and is shown in this 1799 drawing.

The First American Hospital

Many years later, when Franklin had become wealthy, he was approached by one of his colleagues from the American Philosophical Society—an American doctor named Thomas Bond, who had studied medicine in France and England. Bond had observed that the medical care in Europe was better than the medical care in the colonies. When he returned to Pennsylvania, Bond wanted to build a hospital like the ones he had visited in Europe, but he needed to raise the funds in order to pay for it. Thomas talked about his ideas with Ben, who agreed that a hospital would be a great thing for Philadelphia. With Bond's training and Franklin's money, the Pennsylvania Hospital opened in 1752 on Market Street and provided good medical care for everyone, including the poor.

The Freemasons

Although Franklin was glad that he was able to help society through his numerous proposals, he also wanted to do the same for his own social standing. At that time, the finest gentlemen and most successful businessmen in Philadelphia gathered regularly for meetings at a secret club called the Grand Lodge of Free and Accepted Masons, which became known as the Freemasons. Like the Junto, men could join only by invitation, but unlike the Junto, Benjamin Franklin was not invited to join because he was a common tradesman.

Benjamin Franklin was a Freemason who became Grand Master of the Philadelphia Lodge. He is shown in this print at the opening of the Masonic Lodge, wearing the Master's apron.

This group stood for the very things—fellowship, civic improvement, and tolerance—that he did, and the fact that he could not join, did not sit well with Ben. Never one to give up easily, the shrewd Franklin started a campaign to gain membership. First, he printed flattering articles about the Freemasons in the *Gazette*, which did not work. He then ran a long article in which he claimed to have given away some of the group's secrets. Somehow, that worked, and he was invited to join. Not surprisingly, articles in the *Gazette* after he became a member were always positive!

In the course of two years, he became Grand Master of the Philadelphia Lodge. One of the best things about his membership was all the new business it brought him. Whenever one of the members had a printing job that needed to be done, he went to B. Franklin, Printer. As his fortune increased, Franklin was able to spend more of his time writing, which led him to fame far beyond Philadelphia.

Famous Freemasons

The Free and Accepted Masons was founded in London in 1717. Since it began, it has had many well-known and important members. It has also been the subject of many rumors over the years as well. Even today, the Masons meet privately, and have special greetings, ceremonies, and symbols that come from ancient stonecutters' guilds. Benjamin Franklin was just one famous Mason. Others include nine signers of the Declaration of Independence, thirteen signers of the Constitution, and more than thirty U.S. Supreme Court Justices as well as several U.S. presidents, astronaut John Glenn, educator Booker T. Washington, singer Nat King Cole, writer Samuel L. Clemens (Mark Twain), boxer Jack Dempsey, magician Harry Houdini, civil rights activist Rev. Jesse Jackson, aviator Charles Lindbergh, and many more.

In 1734 Benjamin Franklin printed *The Constitution of the Free-Masons.* A copy of the title page is shown here.

not many read the new paper. Franklin stopped printing it after only a few editions.

The failure gave Franklin more time to enjoy his first child with Deborah, Francis Folger, nicknamed Franky. Ben so loved the boy that he had an artist paint a portrait of him. Franky loved Ben, too. When he was old enough, he would follow his father around the printing shop, and watch whatever he was doing.

Francis Folger Franklin, nicknamed "Franky," was the first child of Ben and Deborah together. Ben adored his son, who died at the age of four. This portrait of Franky was actually painted after the death of the young child.

Tragically, Franky died of **smallpox** at age four. For the rest of his life, Benjamin would marvel to friends about what a special child Franky was. His tombstone read, "The delight of all that knew him." About eleven years later, in 1743, Ben and Deborah gave birth to another child—a daughter named Sarah, whom they all called Sally and who became very close to her father.

A Publishing Hit

In late 1732 Franklin printed his first almanac, which became a huge success, and brought him both money and fame. It was called *Poor Richard's Almanack*. An almanac is a book of facts, often including weather predictions, phases of the moon, and other helpful information. It might also include jokes and riddles. Franklin called the author of his *Almanack* "Richard Saunders." Mr. Saunders claimed he had little money, but was very funny indeed. He said he had a wife at home who always wanted more money. It was she who pushed him to write

Poor Richard's Almanack

Ben Franklin's *Poor Richard's Almanack* was not the first American almanac, but it was the funniest, most interesting, and best loved. For twelve years, nearly everyone in the colonies read *Poor Richard's*. They found interesting articles in it, as well as information on legal matters, tips on farming, and new poetry. Of course, a new letter from Poor Richard was in every issue.

But the most popular part of the almanac was the clever **maxims** sprinkled throughout each edition. Many would stand the test of time, such as Franklin's advice that, "early to bed and early to rise, makes a man healthy, wealthy, and wise." These sayings were a mix of Franklin's thinking as well as his own versions of older sayings. Some favorites that people still repeat are: "He that lies down with dogs, shall rise up with fleas." "The sleeping fox catches no poultry." "The worst wheel of the cart makes the most noise." (That last one has become: "The squeaky wheel gets the grease.")

Poor Richard's Almanack was so popular it sold about ten thousand copies each year. In fact, when Benjamin's brother James died in 1735, Benjamin sent his widow five hundred copies to sell, which helped pay her bills.

Poor Richard's Almanack, a title page of which is shown here, was a huge success for Franklin. Practically everyone in the colonies read it not only for its useful information but also for its humor.

Before Franklin started improving the mail system, post offices were set up in colonial pubs and coffeehouses, like the one pictured in this late 19th-century engraving.

was appointed clerk of the Pennsylvania General Assembly. He only received a small salary for the job, but it provided him with the opportunity to print all the papers and money for other colonies.

Then, in 1737, Franklin was made postmaster of Philadelphia. This job gave him a way to get his newspaper to even more readers. Before becoming postmaster, Franklin had to bribe some mail carriers to deliver his newspaper! Now his newspaper could be delivered with the mail.

Franklin had a long history with the postal system in America. In 1753 he was named joint deputy postmaster general for all of the colonies. He lost no time in improving America's post offices the same way he had done in Philadelphia. Before he was

Franklin's Odometer

Franklin always loved to tinker, a hobby that sometimes brought more success his way. In 1762, when he was joint deputy postmaster of the colonies, Franklin invented a neat little tool—the odometer—to help get the mail delivered more quickly. To choose the fastest routes, he needed to know how far one place was from another. The odometer was clipped to the mail cart and counted how many times the wheels went around. Franklin knew how far the cart moved in one turn of the wheel. He then totaled the odometer's reading to figure out how far it had traveled between towns. This helped him find the fastest routes, and greatly improved mail service. Soon, mail got from Philadelphia to New York in a single day!

appointed, slaves, friends, or even sailors carried letters from town to town. Post offices were set up in pubs and coffeehouses. Some letters changed hands many times. A letter to someone in Great Britain often never arrived. Franklin visited every post office to see how it could be made better. He even invented an instrument—the odometer—to help him set up the shortest routes between the colonies so letters could travel more quickly and easily.

CHAPTER 8

Sparks of Invention

[For Benjamin Franklin's] distinguished contributions to experimental science.

— *London's Royal Society*

Ben Franklin loved his work. Writing for his newspaper and printing it were very important to him. But he also pursued another great interest—science. Franklin had a brilliant and curious mind, which led him to one of his greatest triumphs—his insights into electricity.

People in the 1700s were aware of electricity, but they did not know how to use it for anything beyond doing tricks. The most famous of these tricks was performed in the court of the French King Louis XV by physicist Jean-Antoine Nollet, who made 180 soldiers all jump at once when they held hands and Nollet sent a single electric shock through each man. On another occasion, Nollet repeated his joke with seven hundred monks.

Franklin was interested in the effects of electricity. Jean-Antoine Nollet, an 18th-century scientist, conducted experiments with electricity, such as the one shown in this illustration.

Even though these electric experiments amused people, Franklin knew that there was more to electricity than making people jump. The chance to prove it came in 1743, when a Scottish doctor, Archibald Spencer, visited America. Dr. Spencer gave talks on electricity but also used it for pranks. One trick included getting a volunteer's hands and feet to give off sparks. Franklin eventually became Spencer's agent—selling tickets and advertising his show. When Spencer's tour was over, Franklin bought Spencer's tools in order to begin his own experiments with electricity.

Working with Electricity

In 1751, Peter Collinson, an English Quaker who was also very interested in science, wrote to Franklin. Collinson gave Franklin's Library Company a glass tube, along with instructions on how to use the tube for electrical experiments. Franklin was fascinated by the new instrument.

Franklin began his work by studying what electricity was. What were its properties? He began making static electricity. He rubbed the tube with a piece of silk and used the tube to collect the charge. Franklin studied electrical charges for hours on end. The results of his

Franklin devised several uses for electricity. In this 1881 engraving, Franklin and his friends are shown killing 2 turkeys across the Schuylkill River by sending an electrical shock into them.

studies would change the way people saw electricity.

Before Franklin's experiments, scientists believed that electricity was made of two kinds of fluid energy, called "vitreous" and "resinous." Franklin discovered that there was only one kind of electricity, which had an equal positive and negative charge. It became known as the "conservation of charge." Other scientists were impressed by these findings.

Once Franklin learned how to handle electricity, he used it on just about everything. He put a charge on the fence around his house. He even used it on a picture of King George II, so that when anyone touched the king's crown, they got a shock. Franklin called it a "high treason" shock and enjoyed finding victims. However, the fun of shocking people soon wore off, and Franklin realized that he still had not found a real use for electricity, but he was sure that it must be good for something more than jokes.

Franklin studied electrical charges for hours on end.

Franklin kept notes on electricity as he experimented. He wrote, "Electrical fluid is attracted by points. We do not know whether this property is in lightning." Sir Isaac Newton had also believed that lightning and electricity were related but could not explain how. In 1752, Ben Franklin would find out.

Elecrifying Experiments

In 1752, Ben, together with his son William, carried out a secret experiment, using a kite. At the top of the kite was a wire and a little below that was a metal key, The kite wire was tied to a silk ribbon that Ben held. The silk ribbon would keep a strong electric charge from reaching Ben's hand. Armed with this equipment, they waited for a thunderstorm.

Benjamin and his son William are shown conducting an electrical experiment by flying a kite in a lightning storm.

At the first sign of a storm, Ben and his son watched carefully for any sign of lightning. As time and the clouds passed, their hopes faded. Then, suddenly, the kite string began to stiffen. The kite responded to the electricity in the storm, even though Ben and William could not see any lightning.

Reaching up the kite's line, Franklin put his finger on the key. Sparks jumped from his finger into a collecting jar. He raced home to study the sparks in the jar. He found that they had the same properties as electricity, which proved that there is electricity in the atmosphere.

Ben decided not to tell anyone for a while that he and William had carried out these experiments, and did not publish anything about them until months later. Then he printed a letter

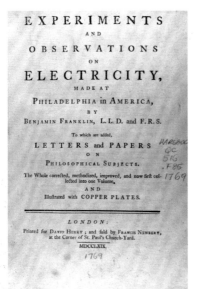

EXPERIMENTS
AND
OBSERVATIONS
ON
ELECTRICITY,
MADE AT
PHILADELPHIA in AMERICA,
BY
BENJAMIN FRANKLIN, L.L.D. and F.R.S.

To which are added,
LETTERS and PAPERS
ON
PHILOSOPHICAL SUBJECTS.

The Whole corrected, methodized, improved, and now first collected into one Volume,
AND
Illustrated with COPPER PLATES.

LONDON:
Printed for DAVID HENRY; and sold by FRANCIS NEWBERY, at the Corner of St. Paul's Church-Yard.
MDCCLXIX.

The title page from the first edition of Franklin's book on electricity is shown here.

to Peter Collinson in his *Pennsylvania Gazette* discussing his findings. Being so hesitant and modest was unlike Franklin, but he may have been worried that his conclusions were not correct.

Franklin need not have worried. Almost as soon as people found out about his discovery, he became famous all over America and Europe. In 1753, Franklin was given the Copley Medal for "distinguished contributions to experimental science," by London's Royal Society.

Ben Franklin wrote a book about his experiences with electricity titled *Experiments and Observations on Electricity, Made at Philadelphia in America*. It would be published in many languages. Franklin was becoming more than a celebrity—he was on his way to becoming a legend.

Lightning Gets Grounded

Today, we know that lightning is electricity caused by a thunderstorm. However, people in the eighteenth century did not. To prevent damaging lightning strikes during storms, churches rang steeple bells to drive the lightning away. Ironically, church steeples were more likely to be struck by lightning, because they were taller than most buildings and had metal bells inside, which would attract lightning.

Ben Franklin thought about the damage lightning did to wooden buildings and ships, and how often it injured people. He experimented with metal and lightning until he found that he could draw lightning to a piece of metal. He then stuck a long rod into the ground. He watched a lightning bolt hit the top of the metal rod and travel through the rod until it went into the ground. Once in the soil, the lightning would lose its force.

He tried out this theory on his house. Sure enough, during the next storm, lightning that struck close to his house was drawn to his "lightning rod" and safely delivered down into the ground.

Soon, lightning rods protected homes, barns, church steeples, and ships. On a ship, the lightning rod would be put on the top of the highest mast. Lightning bolts would hit the rod and travel down the pole without damaging the ship. Many lives were saved because of this simple device.

Because of their height and metal bell, church steeples, like the one shown in this engraving of the "Old Swedish Church in Philadelphia," were often struck by lightning.

A Storm Chaser

In Franklin's day, there was no such term as *storm chaser* (someone who follows thunderstorms). However, Ben was one—very much like storm chasers today, except that he did his chasing on horseback. Ben once chased a whirlwind for almost a mile to see why it spun in a circle.

He made notes of his findings and studied storms and winds. Franklin noticed that a storm in the northeast came from the southwest. He thought it odd that a storm came from the opposite direction of the blowing winds. Franklin kept watching until he noticed that the path of a storm could be plotted.

Franklin began to print the first weather forecasts in his *Poor Richard's Almanack*. His predictions were fairly accurate for the time. Poor Richard said, in the almanac, "Some are weatherwise, some are otherwise." He thought that his readers should be more aware of the dangers of some kinds of weather.

The Franklin Stove

Franklin's curious mind also saw things at home that could be improved. His Pennsylvania fireplace is a famous example. At that time, wood-burning fireplaces in colonial homes were set into a wall and did not allow the heat to spread evenly

Unlike a regular fireplace, the Franklin stove efficiently heated a room. It had an exhaust pipe that let the smoke out of the house and a metal grate that kept the fire going.

throughout a room. Most rooms usually had cold spots in the corners and near the door. In 1744, Franklin came up with a cast-iron furnace that could sit in the middle of a room. The metal soaked up heat from the burning wood inside and warmed the room even after the fire was out. His Pennsylvania fireplace sold well, even though it had a major problem: it did not have a chimney to let smoke out and pull fresh air in, causing the fire to die out quickly.

Franklin's friend David Rittenhouse figured out a way to fix the problem by adding an exhaust pipe that let the smoke rise into the house chimney and then to the outside. Fresh air was able to get into the stove through a special grate and keep the fire alive. This improved stove became known as the Rittenhouse stove and, later, the Franklin stove. Franklin did not **patent** his work. He felt that everyone should benefit from his discoveries.

Franklin and Patents

One of the most telling stories about Benjamin Franklin came at the success of his stove. The governor of Pennsylvania wanted to give him a special patent for his idea, which could have made Franklin a fortune. However, he turned it down so that anyone could copy the stove to make their home more comfortable. Franklin explained his thoughts in his autobiography. He felt that a new invention should be shared with everyone, and that the inventor should be glad to help others.

CHAPTER 9

Trouble with the French and Indians

Join, or Die

Benjamin Franklin was very proud of his scientific discoveries and inventions and of all the improvements he brought to the lives of his fellow citizens. He was now in his late forties, which was considered fairly old at the time. He had worked in the printing business for thirty years, but now he would enter the world of politics and eventually help shape the fabric of American democracy and freedom.

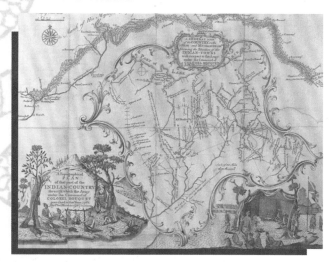

The Ohio River Valley was an important trade area for both the French and the British. This British map of the Ohio River Valley shows the southern shore of Lake Erie in 1764.

In 1748, Franklin was elected to the Philadelphia Common Council; then was named justice of the peace. Three years later, he was elected to the Pennsylvania Assembly, which made laws for the colony. Franklin, later in life, said he was pleased to have such high regard from his fellow citizens. He wrote that he was "flatter'd by all these Promotions . . . for considering my low Beginnings they were great things to me."

Disputes with the French and Indians

At this time in history, there was a long-standing rivalry between the French and the British. Their mutual hatred was old and bitter. Although the thirteen colonies belonged to Britain, there was still a large amount of open land in North America—of particular interest was the Ohio River Valley. This was land that both the British and the French wanted. Whoever held this area controlled trade on the Ohio River, as well as trade with the local Indians, and both countries wanted to claim all the gifts the continent had to offer—the future promise of money, power, and especially, land.

At this time in history, there was a long-standing rivalry between the French and the British. Their mutual hatred was old and bitter.

Caught in this power struggle were the Indians. Both France and Britain wanted to gain their loyalty. Neither country truly cared about their welfare, but instead saw the Indians only as potential partners and soldiers in a possible war.

As an official in Pennsylvania government, Franklin knew that the colony faced some grave threats. One of the biggest was that settlers had to be guarded against attacks by Indians and French explorers. In 1753, Franklin and two other men from

At the Carlisle Conference, Franklin and other representatives met with local Indians to try to stop the mounting tension between the settlers and the Indians. This print depicts a Huron Iroquois village, c. 1500.

Pennsylvania were sent by the colony to the Carlisle Conference to meet with the Indian tribes representing the Six Nations and to convince them to ally themselves with the English. The men bought many gifts of money and goods for them. However, the gifts could not bring the two sides close to an agreement.

The Indians wanted settlers to give back the land they had taken east of the Appalachian Mountains. The Pennsylvanians were not willing to do that. Their best offer was to promise fairer trade. The Indians thought this small offer was an insult. Unfortunately for the British, most Indians sided with the French.

The Albany Conference

Great Britain's dream of a great empire in North America was now in danger. Ben Franklin was among those who believed in this dream. However, he knew that it would take money and arms to win a war against the French. Franklin also knew that the colonies often acted separately from each other. He strongly believed that they would have to unite in order to defeat their common enemy.

The Six Nations

The Six Nations was a collection of six Indian tribes: the Cayuga, Mohawks, Oneidas, Onondagas, Senecas, and Tuscaroras. They lived mostly in New York and were united under one law. When the tribes united is not exactly known, but it was long before Europeans settled in America, perhaps as far back as the 1100s.

The Six Nations had a constitution called *Gayanashagowa*, or "Great Law of Peace." They believed that they were stronger working together than they were separately. The Six Nations still exists today, with more than 80,000 people who claim descent from the original members.

This early 18th-century engraving shows Iroquois leaders from the Five Nations, which included the Cayuga, Mohawk, Oneida, Onondaga, and Seneca. The Tuscaroras later joined the group to comprise the Six Nations.

In the 1700s, the thirteen colonies were united in name under British rule, yet they made their own laws and generally kept to themselves. It was not unusual for one colony to ask its neighbor for help and receive none. Colonists felt it was best to stick to their own business in their own colony. Colonial leaders were too often caught up in their own local problems to see the bigger picture. They left that to Britain.

Ben Franklin argued that this kind of thinking would keep America from reaching greatness. Franklin imagined a small group of gentlemen, somewhat like him, plucked from each colony. They would use their collective wisdom to rule on matters that affected all the colonies, and work together to make the colonies whole. As a united force, the colonies would not be so easily attacked by the French.

Britain had already called for men from each colony to meet with men from a group of Indian tribes called the Iroquois nation. Benjamin Franklin was one of them. This meeting took place in Albany, New York.There were two subjects at the Albany Conference that were thought most important. One was how to defend the colonies from the French. The other was how to improve dealings between the British and the Iroquois. Franklin felt that the meeting was the right place to bring up his idea of uniting the colonies for their own safety.

The Albany Plan

Representatives attending the conference did not expect to talk about a colonial union even though others did come with similar ideas. However, not one was as well thought out as Franklin's plan. Ben Franklin suggested that the king appoint a president general to rule, who would be helped by a grand council made up of men chosen by each colony. The president general's duties would include raising an army, keeping peace with the Indians, and proposing laws that would help the colonies.

The members of the conference liked Franklin's idea so much that they decided to formally request his Albany Plan. Excited, Franklin took his plan to the colonial leaders. If they agreed, it would go straight to the British Parliament—the arm of the British government that approves new laws. However, it was not to be. Colonial leaders did not feel the need to unite. In fact, they feared any kind of drastic political change, so they voted down the idea.

Franklin was disappointed by this decision, but was ready to campaign for his ideas. He was becoming an important part of colonial politics, and men in power were suddenly taking note, so he published a cartoon entitled "Join or Die," which concisely presented the options open to the separate colonists.

The First Serious Cartoon

The "Join, or Die" cartoon, created by Ben Franklin for the *Pennsylvania Gazette*, was published on May 9, 1754. It is considered the first published political cartoon.

It was believed at the time that, if a snake was cut into pieces, it could come back to life if it reunited itself before sunset. Franklin showed a snake cut into eight pieces in this cartoon. Seven pieces were colonies, with New England as the snake's head. Franklin used the snake to show his readers how important it was to join together to fight the French before it was too late.

Franklin's "Join, or Die" drawing, which he published in the *Pennsylvania Gazette* in 1754. It encouraged the separate colonies to join together as a single government.

The French and Indian War

The French and Indian War started in 1755, although it was not officially declared until 1756. The odds did not look good for the British. The Indians had sided with the French because they felt that the French had a better chance of winning.

The British soldiers who came to fight in the war were often young men who had recently arrived in America. They were unfamiliar with American land and forests. The Indians took advantage of this weakness and used it to defeat the British. Indian soldiers did not march and shoot in rows like the British did. The Indians seemed to the British soldiers to be everywhere at once. They were behind, beneath, and even above them. The noise, the sting of gunpowder, and the fright of seeing so-called painted warriors up close made the British turn and run in battle after battle.

The war would last for seven years with the English ultimately emerging victorious. For his part, Benjamin Franklin would work to help the cause in his own way . . . by going to England.

In the early stages of the French and Indian War, British forces under General Edward Braddock were defeated at the Battle of Monongahela. Following the death of Braddock, George Washington arrived on the scene as depicted in this 1854 lithograph.

CHAPTER 10

An American in London

[Franklin acts] as if he had been a member of the Royal Family.

—Thomas Penn

As the French and Indian War raged on, there was no end in sight, which raised the important question of who was going to pay for it. In twelve of the colonies, taxes were raised to buy weapons, clothing, and food for soldiers. But the colony of Pennsylvania was different. Unlike the other colonies, it did not belong to Britain. It was known as a **proprietary colony**, and belonged to the Penn family. More than seventy years earlier, King Charles II had given the colony to William Penn to pay off the king's debts. With William gone, his son, Thomas, owned all of it.

Franklin did not approve of a proprietary colony, and he did not like Thomas Penn. Penn did not think much of Franklin, either, calling him a "villain."

In payment for a debt, William Penn obtained the charter rights to some land—which became known as Pennsylvania—from King Charles II in 1681. This engraving depicts William Penn with King Charles II at Whitehall.

He also claimed that Franklin acted "as if he had been a member of the Royal Family." What really angered Franklin was that he could not find a way to bring Penn's rule to an end. Franklin wrote that if he could not gain control of Pennsylvania for the British crown, he would become "a Londoner for the rest of my days."

To London and a New Home

In January 1757, the Pennsylvania Assembly asked Franklin to go to London to meet with British officials, as well as with the Penns and their representatives, who were known as the proprietors. They hoped Franklin, as a **diplomat**, could convince the proprietors to offer Pennsylvanians more rights and greater freedom and to convince King George II and the king's Privy Council to tax their proprietorships. So, in June, Franklin set sail with his son William.

Traveling by sea in the 1700s was often dangerous. Sea captains had to be on the lookout for fighting French and British navies, which was to be expected in a time of war. They also had to be on the lookout for pirates. One stormy night, when the captain was trying to avoid pirates, the ship nearly crashed on the Scilly Islands near the coast of Britain. Luckily, the ship made it to London in one piece. Ben and William Franklin landed in the city where almost thirty-three years ago Ben had left to start his printing business in Philadelphia. London

While living in London, Franklin kept company with Margaret Stevenson and her daughter, Polly, whose pastel portrait is shown here. The Stevensons became Ben's family away from his Philadelphia home.

in the mid-1700s was the second-largest city in the world. Writers and poets, who often spent hours in coffeehouses talking about politics and the arts, made Ben feel welcome.

Franklin had made a strong enemy in Thomas Penn, who was wealthy, intelligent, and stubborn and had no interest in letting a retired printer tell him what to do.

Soon after he arrived in London, Ben found a cozy home away from home. It belonged to Margaret Stevenson and her daughter, Polly. Margaret was a widow near Ben's age. In them, Ben was lucky enough to find a ready-made family. As always, Deborah Franklin stayed at home with their daughter when Ben traveled. She did not share Ben's desire to explore the world. She also did not have Ben's ease with people. The idea of meeting people in faraway lands was more terrifying to her than thrilling. Ben knew that she would be happier to stay at home in Philadelphia.

But Franklin's trip to London was about more than socializing. He had a job to do. In August 1757, Franklin met with Thomas Penn and his brother, Richard. He hoped they could come to an agreement that would allow the Pennsylvania Assembly to have greater control over the colony's future. But, it was not to be. Franklin had made a strong enemy in Thomas Penn, who was wealthy, intelligent, and stubborn and had no interest in letting a retired printer tell him what to do. Thomas Penn and his family made their fortune from Pennsylvania. They were not about to give it up.

Ben Franklin was regarded as a man who could almost always find a way to end a dispute. However, his powers left him when he faced the Penns. Instead, his emotions took over. Ben believed that Thomas Penn was selfish in his treatment of

Pennsylvanians, and was upset that Penn always seemed to win. Ben used his pen to voice his anger. He wrote that he felt "more…contempt for [Thomas Penn] than I ever before felt for any man living." Anger drove Franklin, but it did not help him change the mind of Thomas Penn. Pennsylvania would stay under the Penn family's control until the American Revolution.

Keeping His Cool

While in London, Franklin took a break from politics and renewed his scientific pursuits. He had noticed that he stayed cooler in the summer when he wore light-colored clothes and warmer in the winter when in darker colors. He also noticed that if his summer shirt was wet and a breeze was blowing, he felt cooler yet. Never a person to accept a fact without figuring out *why*, he tried some experiments with John Hadley, a scientist who lived in Cambridge, England, where the two men went to work on this curious phenomenon. By conducting various experiments using a thermometer, they soon discovered the principles of refrigeration.

Never a person to accept a fact without figuring out why, *he tried some experiments with John Hadley . . .*

Another one of Franklin's projects at that time may not have made the world a better place, but it did, at least for a time, make it a more pleasant one. It was called the armonica, which was a musical instrument that made a sound that was said to be "the voice of angels."

Returning to America

Unable to complete the job he had been asked to do, it looked as though Franklin would head home to the colonies.

Discovering the Principles of Refrigeration

On a warm day in 1758, Franklin and Hadley wet the end of a thermometer with ether, a colorless liquid similar to alcohol. Several times, they used a device to blow air on the ether to cause it to evaporate. Each time the ether dried, the temperature on the thermometer dropped. The room was 65 degrees Fahrenheit (18 degrees Celsius). The thermometer they were testing went as low as 7 degrees Fahrenheit (-14 degrees Celsius)! They had done it! The two men had figured out how to cool an item until it was far below the temperature around it. Their work was the beginning of refrigeration as we know it today.

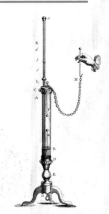

In his refrigeration experiments, Franklin used a thermometer that was similar to the one shown in this engraving.

After all, his wife and daughter were there, and he had already been gone for a year. He wrote to his wife and told her he would return to Philadelphia the following spring. But Franklin was not willing to give up on his Penn mission, and he did not want to go home in defeat. Besides, he was still enjoying his life in London.

By 1762, fighting in the French and Indian War had almost ended, and Franklin felt it was time to go home. It was now almost three years past the time he had promised Deborah he

The Armonica

The armonica was created from the principle that running one's finger around the rim of a glass could make sounds. In 1761, Franklin took that idea a step further. He rigged thirty-seven bowls, each one bigger than the next, to a rod, which was attached to a foot pedal. Pressing the pedal moved the bowls. At the same time, a person ran a finger around the rim of the bowls, which produced a heavenly sound. The armonica was quite popular in its day. French Queen Marie Antoinette took lessons on how to play it, and Beethoven and Mozart composed music for it.

Franklin is depicted here playing his invention, the armonica.

would return. His job as postmaster general and his businesses were becoming too hard to handle from Britain. William Franklin planned to stay in London for a while longer, as he was getting married to an English girl. The couple would later return to New Jersey, where William had been named royal governor.

It was terribly hard for Ben to leave England. He loved it there—the political debates, the opportunity for scientific explorations, the culture, and his happy home with the Stevenson's. His close friends wanted him to run for Parliament, and Franklin gave it serious thought. However, something was pulling him back to the colonies. He set sail on August 24, 1762.

Squabbles Back Home

Back in America, Franklin continued to lose his fight to bring Pennsylvania under the king's rule, but he still refused to back down, mainly because he disliked Thomas Penn, and he was very loyal to Britain. Benjamin relished the idea of taking the colony away from the Penns and giving it to the king.

Franklin felt the only way to win against the Penns was to generate American support—which he tried to get almost any way he could. First, he began a petition to turn Pennsylvania into a royal colony. Then, Franklin and other printers published half-truths about the Penns. They worked crowds of people into a frenzy with—not entirely true—anti-Penn speeches. Perhaps Franklin should have reread some of his own maxims about telling the truth, as his half-truths did not help him garner much support. Colonists who wanted to remain under the rule of the Penn family gained 15,000 signers for their petition. Ben's anti-Penn group raised only 3,500 signers. He had just proven one of his own sayings from the *Almanack:* "Take this remark from Richard poor and lame, whate'er's begun in anger ends in shame."

The fight against the Penns made Franklin an unpopular figure, and in October 1764, Franklin lost his seat in the Pennsylvania Assembly, largely because of his handling of the Penn issue. Franklin was shocked. How could he have lost his seat? Franklin's thinking was sometimes clouded by his passion for what he believed was right. However, that did not always mean that he could persuade others to share his views. It would be a struggle that he would face again and again in the coming years.

Based on Franklin's observations and findings, this Gulf Stream chart was created in the 19th century.

A Return to England

The loss of his seat in the Assembly gave Franklin all the reason he needed to return to England. Once again, Deborah refused to travel with him. She would instead stay to watch as their large new home was being built on Market Street, steps away from where she first saw the awkward young Ben arrive in Philadelphia. After Ben sailed for London, she would never see him again.

Although Franklin had much on his mind, it never stopped him from looking at the world in new ways to improve it. As Benjamin spent time at sea, he became interested in the ocean and sea travel. For example, he wondered why it was faster to sail from America to Europe than from Europe to America. The trip east took two weeks less than the one west.

Ben's cousin, a whaling captain named Timothy Folger, told Ben that the difference was due to a warm current that ran like a river through the Atlantic Ocean. This current, known as the Gulf Stream, moved east at about three to four miles per hour. It was a great help to a ship heading toward England, but would slow a ship sailing to America.

As Ben sailed the Atlantic, he used a thermometer on a rope to take the water temperature several times a day. He also noted the strength of the winds. His notes, along with a map of the

Franklin's Home

The brick house that Franklin built on Market Street was the only house he owned. It was built between 1763 and 1765 and was three stories high. Because he was away much of the time in Europe, he did not spend a lot of time there. After his final return from France, at the age of eighty, he expanded the house so he could have a library. He would say, "I hardly know how to justify building a Library at an age that will so soon oblige me to quit it."

The house was torn down in 1812, but today, Franklin Court, which is located on Market Street between 3rd and 4th Streets in historic Philadelphia, is a tourist attraction with a "ghost" beam structure that outlines Franklin's original house and has an underground museum that displays interactive exhibits about Franklin.

Today, Franklin Court in Philadelphia attracts thousands of tourists who want to see where the great Benjamin Franklin worked and lived.

Gulf Stream that Folger drew, were printed in London in 1769. They were used as a guide to help ships' captains sail this "warm river" on their trips east. The tools and methods Ben and Timothy used were very simple. Yet, their map of the Gulf Stream is so accurate that it was used for many years.

Cause for a Cold

While in London, Franklin came up with some insightful observations and theories with regard to the common cold. Most people at that time thought that catching a chill caused a virus. Franklin was one of the first people to propose that viruses might not come from cold winter air but "may possibly be spread by contagion." He suggested that people wash their hands more often to keep from passing viruses from one person to another.

Franklin often traveled in the middle of winter in unheated coaches. He said, "I have often suffered cold sometimes . . . only short of freezing, but this did not make me catch cold." He told a friend that he thought people often catch a cold from others when shut up in small rooms. It would take another 150 years before Franklin's idea was proven. In 1914, a German professor showed that viruses moving from one person to another spread cold germs.

During the winter months, Franklin may have bundled himself in warm, fur-lined clothing, but he believed illnesses like colds were spread through contagious viruses, not the cold winter air.

CHAPTER 11

Taxation Without Representation

No; they will never submit to it.

England was changing. They had won the French and
Indian War and signed the Treaty of Paris in 1763—
formally defeating the French. The British Empire gained
much of the land it had wanted—all of Canada and the
whole east coast of America, except what is now Florida.

This French map from 1755 shows what lands the French and English
possessed at the start of the French and Indian War. After winning the war,
England gained new territories in Canada and America.

But there was a problem that came with all this new land—it had to be protected. Soldiers were needed to guard it, and those soldiers needed food, clothing, horses, cannons, and other weapons. Shipping all these supplies to America was costing Britain a great deal. The country's debt had already risen to 137 million pounds. Britain needed cash—right away.

Outrage over the Stamp Act

To raise some of this money, the British government decided to force a new tax on the colonists. After all, it was their land that had cost so much money to win and protect. Surely they would see the importance of helping to pay for it. The new tax, called the Stamp Act, was on a basic, necessary item—paper. The tax applied to all paper goods—writing paper, newspapers, books, even playing cards. The British thought this was a fair way to get more money from the colonies. They could not have realized how angry Americans would become over the Stamp Act.

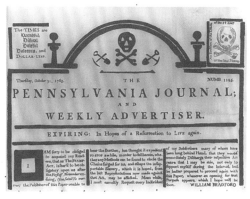

Colonists were angered by the Stamp Act. Publications such as this one from *The Pennsylvania Journal* carried cartoons and articles opposing the new law.

The colonists were particularly angry because it taxed paper, which was a common, everyday need for most people. Paper was also a material that was made in, and used in, the colonies. Before this, taxes were only paid on goods sent to Britain in trade. This new kind of tax meant that the government in Britain could now make money on goods that did not even involve them.

Americans were not only angry about the type of tax they were asked to pay. They were even more upset that the British government ruled to tax them without their consent. Americans had no representation in Parliament—no one was looking out for their rights. No one was there to speak for them. The cries of "No taxation without representation!" rang throughout the colonies.

Throughout the colonies, mobs demonstrated against the Stamp Act. In this 19th-century engraving, an angry group in New York City is shown railing against the new act.

Walking a Fine Line

Still in England, Ben Franklin walked an invisible, fine line between being British and being American. This gave him a special understanding of both worlds, but it also made it hard for him to fully side with either. Franklin did not think the Stamp Act was right, but was not as angry as other colonists, perhaps because he had lived seven of the previous ten years in England, and understood the British position a bit better than the average colonist.

As soon as the Stamp Act was passed in 1765, the Pennsylvania Assembly passed a declaration saying that its citizens would not pay. Franklin, on the other hand, underestimated American outrage. He said that they would not be able to win this battle, and should pay without argument. This angered the colonists, who felt Franklin had betrayed them. A mob tried to destroy his Philadelphia home and was stopped only when his supporters blocked the way. However, the damage to his reputation had already been done. America, it seemed, had turned its back on Ben Franklin.

Repealing the Stamp Act

In October 1765, the Stamp Act Congress, a group of representatives from nine colonies, met at Federal Hall in New York City. This congress was the first step toward the American Revolution, and it was the first time since the Albany Congress—eleven years earlier—that Americans united to work together for their common benefit. After two weeks of discussion, the representatives issued a statement saying that the Stamp Act must be undone, or repealed. It said that Britain had no right to tax the colonies at all—ever.

This 1797 lithograph shows Federal Hall, where the Stamp Act Congress met in October 1765 to try to find a way to repeal the Stamp Act.

Realizing his earlier error, Franklin threw himself into the efforts to repeal the tax and appeared before Parliament in 1766 to explain the colonists' position. He was asked if a modified Stamp Tax would be agreeable. Franklin answered, "No; they will never submit to it." Members of Parliament then asked if he thought any other tax could be put on the colonies. He simply said, "They would not pay it." Less than a week later, the Stamp Act was repealed, and Franklin was back in America's good graces.

It was 1767, and Ben Franklin was on top of the world once again. His reputation was restored, and he felt that Britain and America could now put the problems of the Stamp Act behind them and move ahead as partners. He refused to believe that Britain and America would grow apart. The Stamp Act had been repealed. Still, neither country trusted the

Less than a week later, the Stamp Act was repealed, and Franklin was back in America's good graces.

other. Britain was like the stern parent, and America responded as the angry teenager.

Ben Franklin seemed to act as the referee between the two and a cheerleader for both. His background as a writer had helped him to see both sides of almost any quarrel. His personality made him a natural problem solver, but the time for solutions was drawing to a close.

Caught Between America and England

In June 1767, Americans were again angry about taxes on imported goods like tea, glass, paint, and paper. This time they were called the Townshend Acts. Americans were now bitter, and did not want any tax from Britain, especially since they still had no voice in Parliament. A **boycott** began of all British goods.

Franklin tried to calm the Americans from England, asking them to display "civility and good manners." He also tried to reassure the angry British. Franklin wrote an essay for the British newspapers in which he tried to get them to see the American point of view.

Even Franklin was beginning to see now that taxation without representation was a stumbling block that could not be moved. He wrote a letter to his son William, saying that the more he thought and read about the problems between the two countries, the less he could see how to fix them.

A Division in the Family

In Philadelphia, Deborah Franklin missed her husband. "I stay at home and flatter myself that the next packet will bring me a letter from you," she wrote to Ben. His responses were never quite as heartfelt. Though Ben would hint at returning home, he would not do so for some time to come. When Sally, their daughter, became engaged to Richard Bache in the summer of 1767, Ben wrote to Deborah, "I doubt whether I

'TWAS ENOUGH TO VEX
THE SOULS OF THE MEN OF BOSTON TOWN,
TO READ THIS UNDER THE SEAL OF THE CROWN.

TAX·ON·
TEA·
3ᵈ per lb

THEY WERE LOYAL SUBJECTS OF GEORGE THE THIRD,
SO THEY BELIEVED AND SO THEY AVERRED,
BUT THIS BRISTLING, OFFENSIVE PLACARD SET
ON THE WALLS, WAS WORSE THAN A BAYONET.

England passed the Townshend Act in 1767, which taxed imported goods such as tea. This political cartoon shows an American colonist reading about the new tax while armed British soldiers stand nearby.

shall be able to return this summer. I would not occasion a delay in her happiness if you thought the match a proper one." Deborah replied sharply. "I feel obliged to be father and mother. I hope I act to your satisfaction, I do so according to my best judgment."

Ben did not return that summer to see Sally be married. Instead, he divided his time between Mrs. Stevenson's home and a vacation in France. When Polly married in 1770, Ben walked her down the aisle. Surprisingly, he would go to neither of his own children's weddings. Deborah felt his absence, and, at sixty years old, felt that her chances of seeing Ben again were fading. "I am in the dark and my life of old age is one continued state of suspense," she admitted. She never stopped asking Ben when he was coming home.

He finally wrote that he did not want to go back to America. "I shall find myself a Stranger in my Own Country . . . it will seem like leaving Home to go there." Deborah understood. She wrote one last letter to Ben and died a year later, in December 1774. Ironically, Ben, growing increasingly worried about her, wrote Deborah many letters before he heard about her death.

Sarah Franklin was the youngest child of Benjamin and Deborah. She married Richard Bache and had seven children. Together they took care of her father in his old age and inherited most of his estate.

On his trip to Ireland in 1771, Franklin witnessed the poverty of that country, which was ruled by King George III— the monarch of Great Britain and Ireland.

Franklin Visits the Emerald Isle

In 1771, Ben toured Ireland, another country under British rule. His trip began as a vacation to Dublin—and also to see what kind of help American colonists might expect from the Irish. Later, he decided to travel into the countryside, and what he saw there horrified him.

The country people of Ireland were terribly poor. Whole families ate absolutely nothing but potatoes and buttermilk—even

. . . most of the crops grown by the Irish were taken by the British to feed their own people.

for breakfast. They blamed England for the way they had to live their lives, because most of the crops grown by the Irish were taken by the British to feed their own people.

Ben quickly saw that, if it chose to, Britain could do the same to the American colonies as it had done to Ireland. His feelings about Britain were beginning to change.

Irish Poverty

By the time Franklin visited Ireland, British absentee landowners owned much of the farmlands there. Irish farmers worked as tenants on the land and had to pay a rent to farm the land. Over the course of several years, the wealthy landowners would subdivide what little land a tenant had in order to allow other tenant farmers to work the land and to collect more rent. Some families were only allowed an acre or less to live on and were charged higher rents for smaller parcels of land.

The tenant farmers and their families lived in mud cabins without any windows and barely had chairs and beds to sleep on. Often times, their farm animals shared their quarters. Since potatoes were the main crop in Ireland, many of the farm families lived solely on potatoes and had very little, if any, meat to eat.

Much of these poverty conditions that Franklin observed could be traced back to the laws that the English established for the Irish.

CHAPTER 12

Declaring Independence

Yes, we must indeed all hang together, or…
we shall all hang separately.

As feelings between America and Britain became even more strained, Parliament worked to find a compromise. It even suggested removing the tax on everything but tea, which seemed like an excellent bargain to the British. Franklin, still in London, predicted, "It's not the sum paid in that duty on tea that is complained of as a burden, but the principle of the act."

Despite the quarrel between Britain and America, Franklin was as popular as ever, and might have been the most famous American in the world. He wrote to his son that his company was so desired that he rarely ate at home, and was always invited to visit friends' homes. Franklin enjoyed being a celebrity.

In 1773, colonists were angry about tea. That year, Parliament passed the Tea Act, which gave the East India Company the sole right to sell tea in America. Even though the price of tea fell as a result of the act,

Even though Franklin was at odds with Britain's actions, he was a very popular figure in England. This 1877 engraving shows Franklin meeting with William Pitt the Elder, a member of Parliament, in 1775.

This 19th-century engraving depicts the Boston Tea Party of 1773, when the Sons of Liberty dressed up as Indians and dumped hundreds of crates of tea into Boston Harbor in protest of the Tea Act.

Americans had had enough and decided to take action. On the night of December 16, 1773, a rebel group called the Sons of Liberty dressed up as Mohawk Indians and boarded three ships that were anchored in Boston Harbor. These ships were loaded with East India Company tea and the "Indians" dumped all 342 crates of tea into the harbor. This incident became known as the Boston Tea Party.

Time to Take Sides

In January 1774, Franklin was called before the king's councilors, and was made the **scapegoat** for the problems between Britain and America. When the meeting was over, Franklin was no longer postmaster general. Britain had turned its back on its strongest American defender. However, Franklin did not leave right away for America. He tried to save the link between Britain and her colonies, even offering to cover the cost

This 1859 engraving shows Ben Franklin standing before the Lords of the Privy Council in London in 1774. They came to blame him for the troubles between Britain and America, and in 1775 Franklin returned to America.

of the tea destroyed during the Boston Tea Party. Nothing worked. On March 20, 1775, Benjamin Franklin set sail for home as an American **patriot**, not a British subject.

It was May 5, 1775, and Ben Franklin was sixty-nine years old. He would not let his age slow him down—or keep him quiet. The day after he returned to America, Franklin was asked to join the Second Continental Congress, which had been formed to discuss the Battle of Lexington and Concord, which marked the start of the Revolutionary War.

Franklin was one of the most respected men in the congress. His

> *On March 20, 1775, Benjamin Franklin set sail for home as an American patriot, not a British subject.*

support of the American cause sometimes made Ben's letters to his English friends seem confusing. In one letter, he ranted about how Britain was evil and corrupt, then politely asked how his friend's young daughter was. He knew that there was a difference between a country's government and its citizens.

Trouble Between Father and Son

William, Ben's oldest son, was a victim of Franklin's personal war against Britain. Young William had been Ben's favorite companion, a partner in his electricity experiments, and had traveled with him all over Europe. William had even been named royal governor of New Jersey by the British government.

Benjamin's son, William, was a British loyalist who supported the English in America's fight for independence. This 19th-century engraving depicts William being arrested by American soldiers.

Ben expected William to step down from his post and join in the fight for independence. He would not. William felt his duty was with the British, which his father saw as both disloyal and embarrassing. With war looking certain, Ben wrote to warn William to change sides, signing the letter coolly, "B. Franklin." Benjamin and his son never reconciled, and Ben would leave his son almost nothing in his will. For his part, William gave Franklin a grandchild—William Temple Franklin.

The Declaration of Independence

Most Americans felt that their problems were with the British Parliament. Like Franklin, they did not blame the people of Britain or their king. The Second Continental Congress had to convince the American people that they had to be free of Britain in order to become a great country.

A smaller group was chosen to tell Great Britain, in writing, what America wanted, and was willing to fight for. The most important request was independence from Britain. This committee included Ben Franklin, John Adams, Roger Sherman, Robert Livingston, and Thomas Jefferson. Jefferson would write the first draft of the document, which became the Declaration of Independence.

Jefferson's writing style was different from Franklin's. Though Franklin only made small changes, one has stood the test of time. In the original draft, Jefferson wrote, "We hold these truths to be sacred and undeniable." Franklin crossed out the last three words and replaced them with, "We hold these truths to be self-evident."

The Second Continental Congress agreed to the Declaration of Independence on July 4, 1776. It was then sent to a nearby print shop, where about two hundred copies were printed. One copy was sent to George Washington, now the leader of the Continental army. The general had it read to his troops as a way to raise their spirits as patriots. Another copy went to Britain as soon as a ship could get it there.

At the Second Continental Congress, George Washington was named Commander in Chief of the Continental Army as depicted in this 1876 lithograph.

John Hancock signed the Declaration on August 2. He said, "There must be no pulling different ways. . . . We must all hang together." Franklin then added, "Yes, we must indeed all hang together, or . . . we shall all hang separately."

As commander of the Continental army, George Washington is shown reading the Declaration of Independence before his army in this illustration by Howard Pyle.

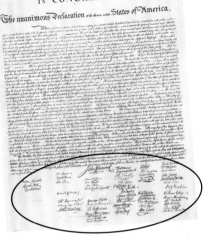

There were 56 signers of the Declaration of Independence, including Benjamin Franklin from Pennsylvania and two future presidents, John Adams and Thomas Jefferson.

The Declaration of Independence reached Great Britain in late 1776. Americans had truly washed their hands of the king and of Parliament. The congress began taking further steps to make America a truly separate country. It started its own post office, and Franklin was named postmaster general. It also started to form its own government.

America's first try at a central government was laid out by the Articles of **Confederation**. It called for a number of new laws, including one allowing freedom of movement, which meant that anyone could travel from state to state. Another was that each new state would have one vote in the new congress.

Against the objections of Benjamin Franklin, the bald eagle was chosen as the new nation's symbol. It looked strong and fierce, so it seemed like the perfect emblem for a small, new country that was fighting a war against the strongest army in the world. The bald eagle was soon seen everywhere.

Franklin's Choice for the Nation's New Symbol

Franklin wanted to use the American turkey rather than the bald eagle as the nation's symbol. He felt the turkey was a "much more respectable bird."

Ben Franklin did not think much of the eagle, and did not want it used as a symbol of the new United States. He said that, "I wish the Eagle had not been chosen the representative of our country. He is a bird of bad moral character. He does not get his Living honestly. . . . Besides he is a rank coward. . . . He is therefore by no means a proper emblem for the brave and honest [people] of America. . . ."

"I am [more in favor of] a Turkey. . . . The Turkey is in comparison a much more respectable bird. . . . He is besides, though a little vain & silly, a bird of courage, and would not hesitate to attack a [soldier] of the British Guards who should presume to invade his farmyard with a red coat on." Franklin may have been right about which bird had more courage, but he was outvoted. The eagle became the new country's symbol.

The bald eagle was chosen as the new nation's symbol. Shown is the Great Seal of the United States.

CHAPTER 13

Life in France

I have at the request of friends sat so much and so often to painters . . . that I am perfectly sick of it.

Americans were now trying to build a new nation and fight a war at the same time. They needed all the help they could get. They looked to Britain's most hated enemy—France—to take up their cause in late 1776. Congress sent a group of men to France to convince the French to fight on the American side in the Revolution.

With the American War of Independence started, Franklin was sent to France to gain their support against England. A 19th-century engraving shows Benjamin Franklin in the court of King Louis XVI of France.

Franklin was one of those chosen to meet with the French king, Louis XVI. Franklin was an old man now, especially by colonial standards. He suffered from a number of painful ailments. Still, he was excited to be chosen and brought his quick wit and brains to the group. He also brought along his two grandsons, sixteen-year-old Temple Franklin (William's son), and seven-year-old Benjamin Franklin Bache (Sally's son).

He was already respected as a writer and scientist and the French much admired Franklin's thinking.

When Benjamin Franklin arrived in France to negotiate help for the American Revolutionary War, his fame had preceded him. He was already respected as a writer and scientist and the French much admired Franklin's thinking. They also deeply respected what he and America stood for: enlightened thought, inalienable rights, and equality.

For his part, Franklin was happy just to be in France! He loved the courtly French way of life. Franklin's image was seen all over France. His face was painted on cloths, dishes, jewelry, and chamber pots, which were eighteenth-century toilets that were often highly decorated. Franklin was so beloved by the French people that his portrait hung in many homes.

In a letter to his daughter, Sally, Ben told her that his image was all over France. It made him realize that his face was now "as well known as the moon." In a letter he wrote to her later, he also complained about having to sit still for a long time while a new portrait was painted. "I have at the request of friends sat so much and so often to painters . . . that I am perfectly sick of it." Nonetheless, he did it.

Although British commander General Charles Cornwallis sent his second-in-command to the surrender at Yorktown, Cornwallis is depicted in this lithograph c. 1845, surrendering to General George Washington at Yorktown, Virginia. That battle marked the end of the war.

Keeping His Eye on the Prize

With all of his social status and fine living in France, Franklin never forgot why he was sent there. There was no way that Americans could win the war without French support. The young nation did not seem strong enough to beat the British army. Franklin worked his magic. Slowly but surely, Franklin gained not only money but weapons and military help to fight against the British in America. By the end of the war, France would spend more than one billion livres ($125 million) for the American cause.

In 1781, the British army under Lord General Charles Cornwallis surrendered. America's independence was almost won. The last thing it had to do was to settle a treaty with Britain, which would spell out what America would gain from its victory.

The Treaty of Paris officially ended the war on September 3, 1783. It recognized the thirteen colonies as thirteen "free and **sovereign** States." Together they became known as the United States of America. Benjamin Franklin was one of the signers.

Spring Ahead, Fall Back

Although Franklin's main reason for being in Paris was to gain support for the American cause against the British (which he succeeded in doing), he could never stop thinking about how to make anything and everything around him better.

Daylight Saving Time

Daylight saving time is used in spring and summer when the days are longer. The clock is set ahead one hour. People get up at the same time as they did before, but they have an extra hour of light at the end of the day. When the days get shorter again, in the fall, the clocks are turned back to standard time. Daylight saving time was first observed in the United States in 1966. Today, Arizona and Hawaii are the only two states that remain on standard time all year long.

Franklin was one of the first supporters of starting the day earlier to take advantage of the early rising sun in the spring and summer. To achieve this, the hands of the clock, such as the one on this 18th-century Swedish clock, would be moved ahead one hour, then moved back for the fall and winter.

One late night in Paris, while playing a lengthy chess match, Ben was astonished to find that it was already light out. Although he was the man who wrote, "Early to bed and early to rise makes a man healthy, wealthy, and wise," he did not always follow his own advice later in life. Ben checked his watch and found that it truly was six o'clock in the morning. He thought that it was odd that the sun should rise so early, and was astonished that he had never noticed before when the sun rose in the winter months. He began to think about how people might get up earlier, and take advantage of the "extra" daylight.

Finally, Franklin published this idea in a light, funny article for a Paris newspaper in 1784. He even mentioned not paying much attention to the sunrise tables in his own *Almanack*! However, Franklin did really think that it would be best for people to start their day earlier, while there was already sunlight. They could get more work done and burn fewer candles at night. The candlemaker's son figured out that if people would start their days with the sun at this time of year, Paris would save 96,075,000 livres. "An immense sum," Franklin wrote, somewhat jokingly. Although some people were intrigued by these ideas, it would not be until World War I that Franklin's idea would lead to what we now know as "daylight saving time."

Rising Hot Air

While living in France, Franklin saw the world's second hot air balloon flight on August 27, 1783, along with thousands of other people, at a field in Paris. Franklin was very interested in the idea of air travel. He made some predictions for the future of flight. Franklin thought that hot air balloons would become more than just a fad. According to him, hot air balloons would be used

In 1783, Franklin witnessed a hot air balloon flight in Paris and predicted correctly that these types of balloons would eventually be used for military spying as well as to gather weather information.

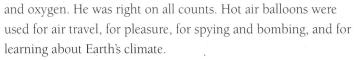

by the military in the future to spy on enemies and even to drop bombs on them.

With scientific discoveries always in the front of his mind, Franklin also suggested that hot air balloons could be used for experiments in the atmosphere to find out more about winds, storms, and oxygen. He was right on all counts. Hot air balloons were used for air travel, for pleasure, for spying and bombing, and for learning about Earth's climate.

Franklin's Voyage Home

It was now 1785, the United States had gained their independence and Benjamin Franklin was ready to return to America. His stay in France had lasted eight years and it was hard for him to leave. In that time, he had made many friends, most of whom begged him to live there for the rest of his life. However, Franklin knew he did not have much time left to live and wanted to return to the new America that he had helped build. America's independence, and Franklin's part in it, was to him "an important Event for the Advantage of Mankind in general."

It was an eight-day trip to the port at Le Havre, where Ben and his grandsons boarded the ship that would bring them home. His work as ambassador was now done. He had made seven voyages across the Atlantic Ocean. This trip home—his eighth crossing—would be his last.

Franklin's Thoughts on Shipbuilding

During Franklin's eight long voyages across the Atlantic, he had sailed through many storms. Some were so bad that the passengers and crew thought the ship would be filled with ocean water and sink. When the weather was calm, Franklin had a lot of time to learn about ships and how they worked. On his last sailing in 1785, he wrote in his journal that Americans should use the Chinese way of building ships, which he had read about. Chinese shipbuilders divided a ship's hold into many watertight parts instead of one open hold that ran the length of the ship. If water filled one hold, it could not spread throughout the ship and sink it. Ships today are still built with this plan of many watertight holds to protect them against sinking.

The hold of a ship is where cargo and other equipment are stored. As a precautionary measure, Franklin encouraged American shipbuilders to build separate holds—as seen in the cutaway drawing of this 18th-century ship—that were watertight.

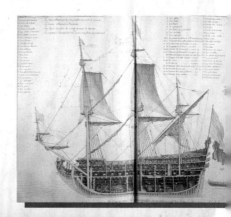

CHAPTER 14

The Printer's Story Ends

The noblest question in the world is What good may I do in it?

When he returned to Philadelphia, Franklin was greeted by many people, who were happy to see him. "An affectionate welcome," he recalled, that "was far beyond my expectations." With Benjamin Franklin gone, the job of ambassador to France was passed to Thomas Jefferson, who had been the U.S. Minister to France. Jefferson had a sharp mind and a warm personality. Like Franklin, Jefferson had a love of music, culture, and most important, the French.

Upon returning from France, Franklin was warmly greeted by family and friends. He was met with a sedan chair and two porters who would carry the elderly statesman home.

In 1787, Franklin was one of 39 members to sign the U.S. Constitution. Franklin can be seen seated up front in this painting by Howard Chandler Christy.

Even in his very old age, Franklin was a busy man. He started work again on the autobiography he had started writing years earlier and was elected president of the state of Pennsylvania three years in a row, the limit that one person could serve. In one of his final acts as a statesman, Benjamin Franklin, already eighty-one years old, was chosen as a delegate to the Constitutional Convention, which gathered to draft a constitution for the new United States of America. His health was failing, but Ben was not about to miss this momentous occasion.

Although his participation in the debates was limited, he provided a calming presence to the other members. On September 17, 1787, Franklin joined thirty-eight other delegates and signed the newly drafted U.S. Constitution. Franklin was one of a handful of delegates to have signed both the Declaration of Independence and the Constitution of the United States.

Seeing Things Clearly

Ben Franklin lived for a long time and was part of many changes in the world. But one of the problems of growing old in the late eighteenth century was that medicine was not yet able to help most of the ailments that plagued the elderly. Painful conditions like pleurisy and kidney stones bothered Ben all the time. He sometimes had to be carried to meetings.

Ben did, however, find a way to help his fading sight. He had two pairs of eyeglasses. One was for looking at things close to his face, such as books, newspapers, and diplomatic papers. The other pair was for looking at people, and things farther away. Ben hated the constant switching back and forth between glasses, and put his inventive mind to work yet again.

He had each pair of lenses cut in half. The halves used for things far away were put in the top half of the eyeglass rims. The reading halves were put in the bottom of the same rims. "By this means . . . I have only to move my eyes up or down, as I want to see distinctly far or near, the proper glasses always being ready." These glasses, known as bifocals, are still worn today.

In this illustration, Franklin is shown wearing his glasses and looking over his drawing of the bifocal he invented for seeing up close and far away.

Franklin Makes His Arm Longer

When Franklin finally retired from Pennsylvania politics, he had even more time for inventing. As an old man, he was having trouble getting in and out of chairs and climbing his chair stool, which he had previously desinged. He needed a different kind of help to reach for books in the upper shelves of his library. His grandchildren were happy to climb up on his stool to get his books for him, but they were not always there to help. To help him reach books that were too high up, Franklin invented a longer arm called an "extension arm."

This tool was a long wooden pole that had two metal attachments at the end, like fingers. These fingers could be opened or closed by pulling on a cord tied to them. Franklin could reach up with the pole, open the fingers at the end of it, and close them around the book he wanted. The extension arm allowed Franklin to reach three feet higher than he could before. Many devices like this one are made today to help people reach objects on high shelves.

Communicating Ants

In his retirement, Franklin also had more time for observing nature. One day, Ben went into his kitchen for some food. Someone had left a small pot of molasses open on a shelf, and the jar and shelf were covered with ants. Because molasses was expensive, he picked up the pot and shook out the ants rather than throw the whole thing away. Only one ant remained inside the pot and kept eating.

In his retirement, Franklin also had more time for observing nature.

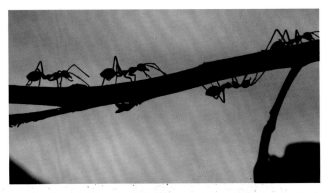

Franklin often used the scientific practice of observation to come to certain conclusions. Upon watching ants marching in a line on numerous occasions, he concluded that ants communicate with each other in some fashion.

Watching the single ant, he wondered if ants could communicate, or if they just followed the lead ant wherever it went. It was time for another experiment. Franklin tied a string around the rim of the molasses pot, tied the string to a nail he put into the kitchen ceiling, and hung it from the ceiling. Eventually, the ant that was left in the molasses came out of the pot, to the rim. It crawled down the side of the pot, looking for the shelf the pot had rested on. Once the ant found no shelf, it went back up the jar, around the rim, and up the string to the ceiling. It then seemed to follow the original path the ants took across the ceiling to reach the shelf and went down the wall and outside through a crack in the wall.

Franklin continued to wait. Within a half hour, there was an army of ants coming into his kitchen. They marched up the wall and across the ceiling to the string again, using the same path that the last ant took as it had left. Soon, Franklin was watching two lines of ants: One went down the string to the molasses. Another line of ants, which had eaten as much as it could, went up the string, across the ceiling, and outside to its nest again. This continuous march did not stop until the molasses jar was empty.

Through his observation, he concluded that ants did communicate. It was obvious to him that the one ant had let the others know that food was to be found, where it was, and how to get it. Since that time, many scientists have studied ant behavior, and confirmed Franklin's findings.

Franklin's Stand on Slavery

During the eighteenth century, slavery was a common practice in the United States. Franklin was no different from most men with money—he owned slaves. This was not something that troubled him as a younger man. But later in life, the irony of fighting for independence, while at the same time owning slaves, greatly bothered Franklin.

The practice of slavery on plantations, like the one shown in this 18th-century engraving, was common during Franklin's days and as such did not bother him. However, after America gained its independence, Franklin came to believe slavery was wrong and worked to get it abolished.

The French Revolution (1789–1799)

During the American Revolution, the French watched with great interest as thirteen colonies fought for independence. The people of France—mainly the lower and middle classes—were dissatisfied with the social and economic conditions of their country and blamed their monarch—King Louis XVI. Bolstered by the American Revolution, they saw how a small group of people could overthrow, and gain their independence from, a mighty country such as England. In 1789 a crowd in Paris stormed the Bastille prison, which was for them a symbol of oppression, then captured and ultimately executed King Louis XVI and his wife Marie Antoinette. For France, the French Revolution was the first step in ridding itself of a system of monarchy. It would take another hundred years before France established a permanent democratic republic.

Like the Americans, the French entered into a revolution to rid itself of an oppressive monarchy. This painting depicts the taking of the Bastille.

He started reading works by **abolitionists**, and he became president of the Society for Promoting the Abolition of Slavery in 1789. He often wrote papers and spoke out against slavery. Sadly, slavery would not end until almost seventy-five years later.

Good-bye to a Great Man

It was April 1790, and Benjamin Franklin was eighty-four years old. That was almost a double life for people of that era. After a lifetime of using his mind and spirit to better his country, the Founding Father was worn out. Years of constant pain and a recent lung infection warned him that the end was near.

At Ben's deathbed were his daughter, Sally, and her husband; grandsons Temple and Benny; and Polly Stevenson, his friend from all those years ago in London. A tearful Sally told her father she wished he would recover and live much longer. "I hope not," Ben replied. He soon died, holding Benny's hand, at 11:00 p.m. on April 17, 1790.

When his death was made public, the world mourned. The French, who began missing him as soon as he had left their country, now wept. A letter sent from the French National Assembly to Congress stated that Franklin's death would be a terrible blow to the French, who were taking their "first steps toward liberty." More than twenty thousand Americans stood on the edges of his city's paved roads to watch his casket go by.

When his death was made public, the world mourned.

Ben Franklin died before he could finish his autobiography. Still, that did not stop it from being printed. After reading *The Autobiography of Benjamin Franklin*, Americans began to better understand and honor the man who had done so much for so many. It has become the most widely published autobiography in history! Ben began it as a letter to William, trying to describe his own life and working-class beginnings. The letter grew as the years passed, and included details of his inventions, beliefs, successes, and struggles.

Today, Franklin is remembered as a great man and a founding father of the United States of America. His portrait appears on the U.S. hundred-dollar bill, and he is one of only two non–U.S. presidents to recieve that honor. The Federal Reserve, using a portrait of Franklin that was painted by Joseph-Siffred Duplessis around 1779, issued the bill in 1914.

B. Franklin, Printer, led a long and eventful life. He was part of the founding of a new country and spent most of his life trying to make the world a better place. He truly lived up to the maxim he wrote years earlier in his *Poor Richard's Almanack*:

> *"If you wou'd not be forgotten*
> *As soon as you are dead and rotten,*
> *Either write things worth reading,*
> *Or do things worth the writing."*

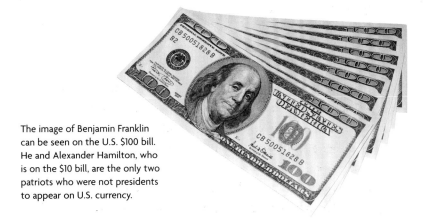

The image of Benjamin Franklin can be seen on the U.S. $100 bill. He and Alexander Hamilton, who is on the $10 bill, are the only two patriots who were not presidents to appear on U.S. currency.

GLOSSARY

abolitionists—people who fought to end slavery.

boycott—to refuse to buy or sell something to a person, company, or country.

Confederation—a group of people, states, or parties united for a common purpose.

diplomat—a person who helps two sides in an argument make an agreement.

franchise—to allow someone else to sell your product for part of the profits.

indenture—a contract requiring one person to work for another for a certain amount of time.

journeyman—a person who has learned a trade and works for another person.

masthead—the top of the front page of a newspaper that shows its name, the date of the issue, and the names of the owners.

maxim—a witty saying that rings true.

patent—a legal document that gives an inventor all the rights to own and control what he or she invented.

patriot—a person (especially a soldier) who loves his or her country and defends it, and tries to make it better.

proprietary colony—one of the original thirteen colonies that was owned by a person or family.

prose—ordinary writing or speech; not poetry.

Puritans—members of a religion that started in England and had strict rules of behavior.

scapegoat—a person bearing the blame for others.

smallpox—a contagious, often fatal disease marked by large blisters on the body.

sovereign—self-governing.

tithe—to pay or give away one-tenth of one's income, especially to support a church.

tract—a pamphlet or leaflet, that is printed about one subject.

BIBLIOGRAPHY

Books

Brands, H. W. *The First American: The Life and Times of Benjamin Franklin*. New York: Anchor Books, March 2002.

Franklin, Benjamin, and Stacy Schiff. *The Autobiography of Benjamin Franklin & Selections from His Other Writings*. Modern Library; new edition, 2001.

Isaacson, Walter. *Benjamin Franklin: An American Life.* New York: Simon & Schuster, 2003.

Morgan, Edmund S. *Benjamin Franklin*. New Haven and London: Yale University Press, 2002.

Wood, Gordon S. *The Americanization of Benjamin Franklin*. New York: The Penguin Press, 2004.

Articles

Herschbach, Dudley R. "Our Founding Grandfather." *Harvard Magazine*, September 2003. http://www.harvardmagazine.com/on-line/090334.html.

Isaacson, Walter. "Citizen Ben's 7 Great Virtues." *Time*, July 7, 2003.

Krider, E. Philip. "Benjamin Franklin and Lightning Rods." *Physics Today*, January 2006. http://www.physicstoday.org/pt/vol-59/iss-1/p42.html.

Lane, Neal. "Benjamin Franklin, Civic Scientist." *Physics Today*, October 2003. http://www.physicstoday.org/pt/vol-56/iss-10/p41.html.

Web Sites

Independence Hall Association in Philadelphia. "The Electric Ben Franklin." Independence Hall Association. http://www.ushistory.org/franklin/index.htm.

Lemay, J.A. Leo. "Benjamin Franklin: A Documentary History." J.A. Leo Lemay. http://www.english.udel.edu/lemay/franklin/.

Lemelson-MIT Program. "The Franklin Stove." Massachusetts Institute of Technology. http://web.mit.edu/invent/iow/franklin.html.

National Park Service. "Ben's Inventions." National Park Service. http://www.nps.gov/archive/inde/Franklin_Court/Pages/franklininventor1.html.

The Franklin Institute. "Benjamin Franklin and His Inventions." The Franklin Institute. http://www.fi.edu/franklin/inventor/inventor.html.

IMAGE CREDITS

ABOUT THE AUTHOR

Maria Mihalik Higgins has been a writer and editor for Rodale Press, Discovery Channel, and U.S. Army Europe in Stuttgart. She is currently director of marketing and corporate communications for a Christian foster care agency in Colorado Springs.

Index